Parents'
Computer
Companion

Parents' Computer Companion

A Guide to Software and Online Resources

Jason D. Baker

Baker Books

A Division of Baker Book House Co
Grand Rapids, Michigan 49516

Published by Baker Books
a division of Baker Book House Company
P.O. Box 6287, Grand Rapids, MI 49516-6287

Printed in the United States of America

Library of Congress Cataloging-in-Publication Data

Baker, Jason D.
    Parents' computer companion : a guide to software and online resources / Jason D. Baker.
        p.   cm.
    Includes bibliographical references.
    ISBN 0-8010-6077-X   (pbk.)
    1. Computers and family. 2. Computer software. 3. Family—computer network resources. I. Title.
    QA76.9.F35B35   1999
    025.04—dc21   99-32104

For current information about all releases from Baker Book House, visit our web site:
http://www.bakerbooks.com

To Julianne
. . . and step by step he'll lead us,
And we will follow him all of our days . . .

For Jamie and Alex

Contents

Acknowledgments

This book would not have been possible without the efforts of some significant people:

Paul Engle, my editor at Baker Book House. Thanks for your continued support, feedback, and patience with my writing efforts.

John McFadden, Tom Podles, and Paul Smith, my various directors at Loyola College. Thanks for your flexibility with my vocational efforts.

Our boys, *Connor and Caleb.* Thanks, Connor, for the daily dose of smiles and laughter. And Caleb, thanks for holding off until this book was finished.

My beloved wife, *Julianne.* The adventure continues . . . thanks for sharing in the journey and making me whole. I love you.

To the only wise God our Father be glory, majesty, dominion, and power both now and forevermore. *Soli Deo Gloria!*

one
Getting Started

During the past decade computers have become an integral part of life for a growing number of people. The explosive growth of the Internet and World Wide Web along with the decline of computer prices have made it increasingly possible to incorporate computers into all aspects of life. In this book we'll explore one type of computer usage that has skyrocketed—educational computing.

A number of quality educational software packages have appeared on the market to promote this growing dimension of the computer industry, and the benefits are evident:

- Educational software and the Internet give students access to a wealth of information that was previously limited to libraries and schools.
- Matching computerized learning experiences with individual learning styles helps students learn more effectively.
- Computers use exploration, problem solving, and synthesis to help students examine the same information from a variety of different angles.
- Students can instantly receive specialized tutoring and reinforcement for difficult subjects and hard-to-master skills.

- Parents and teachers can supplement their own instruction with computer programs and activities.
- Computers allow students to experience environments not otherwise accessible to them (e.g., exploring space, flying a plane, or journeying to a distant land).
- Authoring programs encourage creativity as students compose music, write stories, create movies, and draw artwork.
- Via the Internet students can interact with those they would not normally meet.
- Students of all ages can enroll in complete diploma or degree programs online.
- Students can enhance their computer literacy, an essential skill for the twenty-first-century adult.

Taking the First Step

Despite all of these benefits, educational computing remains inaccessible to many families. Information overload paralyzes many parents: So-called experts tout the computer's benefits, but the vast array of software titles, World Wide Web sites, and computer peripherals are simply overwhelming. Questions are legion: Where do I begin? What kind of computer do I need? What's available on the Internet? What about online dangers? Which software is worthwhile?

This book is written to answer those questions. *Parents' Computer Companion* is designed to introduce you to the world of educational computing. This book is not intended to be exhaustive; it isn't the last word in educational computing, but rather a first word to help you get started. If you can relate to the following situations, this book is for you.

- You're looking to purchase your first family computer and want to know what you need to buy. You'll particularly like the computer and Internet primer in chapter 2.
- After reading about the dangers related to the Internet, you're not really sure if you want to go online. Be sure to examine chapter 3 as we discuss how to child-proof your computer.

- You've had a computer for awhile and have used it for budgeting and sending e-mail. Now you really want to start using it with your kids. Chapter 4 offers practical tips for educational computing experiences.

- It seems that your family wastes lots of time trying to find worthwhile Web sites. Reading chapter 5 will reveal dozens of quality educational online resources for you to explore.

- You've just started homeschooling and are interested in home study opportunities, your child is struggling in school and needs additional tutoring in a specific subject, or you're having so much fun watching your kids learn that you want to continue your own education. Chapter 6 will point you to accredited distance education programs offering courses for kindergarten through graduate school.

- You just want to know how to make wise purchasing decisions. Chapter 7 offers tips on selecting educational software.

- You've already got a computer and want to know which software is worth purchasing for your kids. The recommendations in chapter 8 will guide you.

- You want to know where to find up-to-date reviews and information about educational computing. The last section of this book will point you to additional resources that will keep you current.

Using the computer to enhance your child's education is an exciting experience. I hope you'll find this book beneficial for getting over the initial humps and beginning your educational endeavor. Your children will thank you when you do.

two

Computer and Internet Primer

Before you can begin to explore educational computing opportunities, you need to make sure you have the necessary equipment and online capabilities. If you are new to computers and the Internet, this chapter will help you with your purchasing decisions. If you already own a computer with Internet access, you may want to review this chapter to evaluate whether your current system is adequate.

Choosing a Computer

Because the computer industry changes so quickly, it's virtually impossible to write a definitive guide to purchasing a computer. Computer manufacturers constantly release faster and more powerful machines, more feature-laden software, and new accessories. That means that to stay current you will probably have to replace your computer every two or three years. This can be an expensive process if you're not careful.

As recently as two years ago the target price for a quality family computer was in the $2,000 to $3,000 range. Fortunately, that price has dropped significantly. Multimedia computer systems powerful enough to run ample educational and application software are now available for $1,000 to $1,500, and quality machines priced at less than $1,000 are becoming more prevalent. It is true that the more money you spend, the better computer you will get. But, as we will see, sometimes it is smarter to spend less initially and to save money for a future upgrade.

So what should you look for when purchasing a computer? There are a number of components to consider. Here are my recommendations along with a few words of explanation.

Platform Selection

Both IBM-compatible and Macintosh computers can be high-quality machines. When deciding which kind of computer to purchase, it's important to look at which platform is used on the other machines you use (e.g., at the office and in your child's classroom). For example, if your office and local schools use iMacs, then be sure to follow suit. But because IBM-compatible machines (frequently labeled simply as PCs or Wintel machines) are the most common—even within educational settings—and the largest selection of software is available for this line, many people will find it wise to purchase an IBM-compatible machine.

Processor Selection

The microprocessor is the computer chip that serves as the brain of your computer. There are two things to consider when selecting a processor: type and speed. The most popular processors for IBM-compatible computers are in the Pentium line (Pentium, Pentium II, Pentium III). Macintosh computers use a processor called the PowerPC. Processor speeds are measured in megahertz (e.g., 300 MHz, 400 MHz, 500 MHz). Obviously the best combination is a newer *and* faster processor. But if you must make trade-offs, it's best to select the best processor type rather than simply the fastest speed. Often a newer processor, even at a slower speed, will outperform an older, faster one.

Memory and Hard Drive Space

Bigger is better. The more memory (called RAM) you get, the faster and more efficiently your computer is able to run software. Graphics programs, for example, are particularly memory intensive.

Your hard drive is your storage area for both applications and data. The more programs you plan to install on your computer and the more information you hope to store, the more hard drive space you will need.

Monitor

For many years the only affordable monitors were 14-inch screens, but now most systems come with either 15- or 17-inch screens. If you plan to use your computer for long periods of time, purchase a quality 17-inch monitor. Your eyes will thank you.

Sound and Video

Make sure your system has an AGP video card with 3D acceleration and lots of memory. Your audio card should be a PCI card with 3D audio for best performance. Finally, a set of good quality speakers are important, particularly for programs with spoken instruction. If your computer is in a room where there will frequently be other people, consider purchasing headphones so your child's computer sessions don't disturb his or her sibling's studies.

CD-ROM and DVD

CD-ROM drives are standard on most machines. As with other components, the faster the better for these drives. Speed is particularly vital for reference software that holds most of the material on the CD-ROM. A slow drive will frustrate the learning process.

DVD (Digital Video Disks) are fairly new on the scene though many expect them to replace CD-ROMs in the near future. What makes DVD so significant is that it has the potential to be the all-in-one storage medium. Rather than using videotapes for movies, CDs for music, and CD-ROMs for computers, all three types of information can be stored on DVD. Since DVD drives can read current CD-ROMs, they do offer increased flexibility. But don't feel compelled to spend extra money to add a DVD drive because it will likely be several years before they are commonplace and there are enough programs available on DVD to justify your purchase.

Many people ask whether the preferred delivery medium for software is CD-ROM, DVD, or online. The short answer is that most products currently available on CD-ROM will likely become available on DVD in the coming years. Online software delivery is difficult for large programs because Internet connection speeds are too slow. However, once Internet2 (a higher-speed Internet currently under development) is finished, more software will be available online.

Modem

Most systems come standard with a 56K modem, which is about as fast as you will be able to use with your phone line. Higher-speed Internet access is available through ISDN or cable modems. We'll discuss those options later in this chapter.

Printer

Printers generally come in two varieties: laser and inkjet. If you're planning to do lots of printing (such as if your printer serves double duty with a home business), then a laser printer is a wise investment. The initial cost is higher than for an inkjet, but supplies such as toner are cheaper. Most families, however, will be satisfied with a color inkjet printer. Inkjet printers are relatively inexpensive, produce laser-quality black and white printing, and offer color printing as well.

Other Peripherals

Remember to try out the keyboard and mouse. You'll spend lots of time with them once you get your machine home. Consider ergonomically designed keyboards to reduce hand and wrist strain. A tape backup is another worthwhile investment. It can protect you from losing data in case of a crash. Color scanner prices have dropped dramatically in recent years (down to less than a hundred dollars), allowing you to scan photos, artwork, and other pictures that will enhance your child's learning experience. Finally, don't forget to invest in a good surge protector so that a sudden power surge doesn't destroy your investment.

Tech Support

Quality technical support is vital, and you're more likely to use it than a warranty. You can often measure the difference between good and bad technical support by the amount of time you must spend waiting for a technician to help you. Investigate the options. Call the support line to check out its timeliness prior to making your purchase. Also find out what type of replacement policy is in place for problematic equipment. Some companies deliver replacement parts overnight while others leave you hanging for weeks.

Warranty

A one-year parts and labor warranty is fairly standard, and the minimum that you should expect. This ensures that any equipment problems will be covered by the manufacturer's warranty. Extended warranties are a nice benefit but not worth the additional money.

With all these components to consider, costs can quickly skyrocket if you haven't set a limit for yourself. Therefore, first determine how much you plan to spend. Then choose an appropriate system that fits your budget.

In some cases you may actually spend less than you have budgeted if you avoid paying for features you don't need. The most expensive machine in the store may have a hard drive twice as big as you'll ever use. If so, go for a smaller hard drive and save a few dollars. Remember, too, that spending twice as much doesn't necessarily mean your computer will last twice as long. Over time, new software will demand more than your existing computer can handle. Therefore, while it is important that your computer is powerful enough for current software applications, sometimes it's better to spend less now and to save money for a replacement machine in the future. For example, if you have allocated $2,000 for a computer and hope to get four years of use out of it, you're actually better off purchasing a $1,000 machine now and another one two years from now than simply buying a $2,000 machine.

Peripherals such as printers and monitors don't become outdated as quickly, so they will often last longer than two or three years. Consequently, a more expensive purchase may be worthwhile in these cases because you will be able to use peripherals with multiple machines. My laser printer is now on its third computer.

The bottom line in computer purchasing is to balance budget, current needs, and future potential. Decide what you hope to accomplish with a new computer; then find a machine with the necessary and appropriate capabilities.

Understanding Internet Resources

The use of computers in education is not new; for years schools have maintained computer labs and taught programming classes. The rise of the Internet, however, has pushed technology to the forefront. When the president of the United States calls for every classroom and library in the country to be connected to the Internet and declares that every twelve-year-old must be able to log on to the Internet, it is clear that the Internet is a significant educational resource.

The Internet is a global computer network with an estimated 60 million users worldwide. Originally developed in the late 1960s as a Department of Defense project, it has since moved beyond its government roots. Although it is not owned by any single company, the Internet is now a commercially controlled computer network. Once connected to the Internet, users can choose from a variety of online services including electronic mail, topical discussion groups, and the World Wide Web.

Electronic Mail

Electronic mail is one of the most popular uses of the Internet. A recent study showed that people now use e-mail more often than traditional mail. What makes e-mail so popular is its speed and affordability. E-mail messages travel to destinations around the world in a matter of minutes without incurring long distance charges.

Just as you acquire a street address when you move into a home, you receive an e-mail address when you go online with your Internet Service Provider (more information about Internet

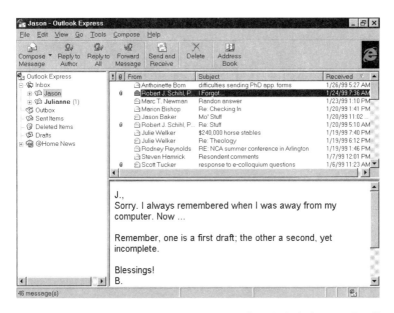

Figure 1: Outlook Express E-mail

Service Providers appears later in this chapter). E-mail addresses consist of a username and domain name connected by an @ symbol. For example, `dav@cts.edu`, `xrwy93a@aol.com`, and `president@whitehouse.gov` are three such addresses.

Sending e-mail is as simple as launching your e-mail program, entering the destination address, giving the message a subject title, and typing your message. The message itself can be as short as a few words or as long as a multiple-page report with attached files.

Unlike the postal service, however, the Internet cannot deliver a message if you make even a minor mistake addressing it. If you type an erroneous destination address, your mail will bounce back to you with a message indicating that either the username or domain name doesn't exist. If you have correct e-mail addresses, though, you can send and receive mail to and from anyone on the Internet, anywhere in the world. This makes e-mail an excellent way to communicate with friends, family, and others.

Discussion Groups

Topical discussions take place throughout the Internet either via electronic mail or a bulletin-board style service called USENET. Electronic mailing lists, sometimes referred to as listservs, are e-mail based discussion groups. Participants subscribe to a particular list and then all contributions to the mailing list are e-mailed to all of the subscribers. This is not unlike the way that memos are distributed within a typical office. While there isn't an exhaustive list of electronic mailing lists, many are cataloged at the List of Lists Web site (`http://www.catalog.com/vivian/inter est-group-search.html`).

USENET newsgroups are the electronic equivalent of bulletin boards—messages are posted at central locations where individuals can visit to browse, search, and respond with their own messages. USENET newsgroups are public discussion areas organized by topic. For example, `rec.music.christian` is a discussion of Christian music while `misc.education.home-school.christian` covers homeschooling from a biblical perspective. With newsgroups you don't have to worry about your mailbox overflowing with contributions that don't interest you. And because they are organized into a central hierarchy, you can easily search for groups that interest you. The downside is that USENET newsgroups are often more chaotic than mailing lists. Because anyone can contribute a message to a newsgroup without having to first subscribe and identify themselves, newsgroups can easily get out of hand.

To conveniently navigate discussion groups, visit the Deja.com Web page (http://www.deja.com). This service archives an entire year of newsgroup postings that you can search by subject, author, or keyword. You can even post new messages to a group from the Deja.com site.

World Wide Web

The World Wide Web is often credited with the recent explosion of the Internet. In fact, most people, when speaking about the Internet, are actually referring to the World Wide Web. The Web is a form of electronic publishing that allows people to publish articles, photographs, sound and video clips, and more in a magazine-like format. It serves as a global electronic library that contains newspapers, magazines, journals, and countless other materials available for perusal. What makes the Web so powerful is that anyone can publish information and interconnect it with other resources already online.

Accessing the Web requires a browser such as Microsoft Internet Explorer or Netscape Navigator. Typically, an Internet Service Provider will provide you with a browser as well as an e-mail program. Figure 2 shows a Web page as seen with the Internet Explorer browser.

Just as everyone with a telephone has a unique phone number, every page on the World Wide Web has a unique address called a Uniform Resource Locator (URL). A URL generally begins with the moniker http:// followed by the address of the page (e.g., http://www.bakerbooks.com). If you know the URL of a particular site, you may access it directly. Fortunately though, you don't need to memorize a list of URLs to visit sites on the Internet. Online directories and search engines allow you to locate interesting places, some of which will be listed in chapter 5.

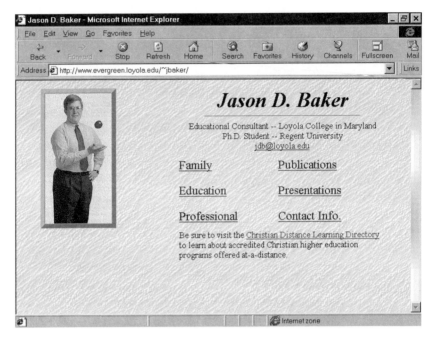

Figure 2: Internet Explorer

The World Wide Web essentially gives families a global library at their fingertips. It also offers people the opportunities to publish personal information, such as family newsletters or student-written articles, and to share it with others online. In the past, parents saved money for sets of encyclopedias for their children. Today money is better spent on an Internet connection; the Web provides many more resources than were ever available in a typical encyclopedia.

As the Web matures, sites have moved beyond simple text and graphics to incorporate animation, interactivity, audio, and video. Such advances often require free plug-in or helper applications. Such applications (e.g., a video player) add functionality that isn't built into your browser. Web sites that use advanced features often give you instructions on how to download and install the appropriate software. Some of the more common applications are as follows:

- Real Player—This program enables you to receive real-time audio and video feeds as well as to play archived clips. Real Player, along with sample audio and video clips, is available online (http://www.real.com).

- Adobe Acrobat—This program makes it possible for documents to look the same on all computers, regardless of the program used to create it. Many brochures and forms are distributed in the Acrobat PDF format. The Acrobat reader can be downloaded from its web site (http://www.adobe.com).

- Macromedia Shockwave—This program makes it possible to view interactive multimedia presentations on the Web. It's often used for online games and animated videos. The Shockwave plug-in is available (http://www.macromedia.com).

Obtaining Online Access

High-Speed Modems

As mentioned earlier, most multimedia computer systems come with 56K modems—the fastest speed you can expect to achieve over your standard telephone line. Because your ability to actually reach 56K speed is dependent on the quality of your phone line, though, many people get connections around only 30K. However, there are some faster alternatives you can pursue if 56K isn't meeting your needs. Three of the more common ones are ISDN, cable modems, and DSL.

ISDN (Integrated Services Digital Network) transmits digital information over standard telephone wire but provides up to a 128K connection. An ISDN connection to the Internet requires a special ISDN modem, an ISDN line from your local phone company, and an Internet Service Provider that supports ISDN. While the installation and equipment costs can total a few hundred dollars, the monthly cost isn't much more than additional phone lines and the ISDN line provides consistent connection speeds two to four times that of standard modems. Check with your local phone company for information about ISDN.

Cable modems, which enable Internet connections at 1500K–3000K using your television cable, offer speeds fifty to a hundred times faster than a typical phone line. When you connect to the Internet using a cable modem, your cable service also serves as your Internet Service Provider. So you don't need to spend additional money for connectivity. Cable modem installation and monthly costs are comparable to ISDN lines but are only available in select areas throughout the United States. Contact your local cable television company to see whether they offer cable modem service.

Digital Subscriber Line (DSL) or Asynchronous Digital Subscriber Line (ADSL) is considered to be the high-speed connection of choice for the near future. It offers high-speed Internet connections (from 256K–7000K) over your standard telephone line using a special modem. One significant advantage over either ISDN or cable modems is that DSL uses your existing phone line for high-speed access. Furthermore, when you are connected to the Internet through DSL you can simultaneously use your telephone or fax machine. Although DSL has a higher initial cost than other options, current monthly prices for DSL are comparable to ISDN and cable modems. Contact your local phone company for more information.

Access Type	Speed	Availability	Installation Cost	Monthly Cost
ISDN	64K–128K	High	$100–$200	$25–$50
Cable Modem	1500K–3000K	Low	$100–$200	$30–$50
DSL/ADSL	256K–7000K	Medium	$400–$600	$40–$150

Since ISDN appears to be declining in popularity while the other two technologies are increasing, your best choices for high-speed access are either cable modem or DSL. The best bet is to check pricing and availability in your area, find out what experiences your friends have had, and choose whatever seems best.

Internet Service Providers

To access the Internet, you will need an Internet Service Provider (ISP). There are literally thousands of ISPs scattered around the world. Some, such as America Online, offer significant amounts of proprietary online material in addition to access to the Internet. Others, including local providers and national providers such as AT&T WorldNet, provide full Internet access with varying degrees of proprietary information in return for a cheaper monthly rate. Finally, some providers such as Juno offer limited Internet access for free. Let's look at some of the aforementioned leaders.

America Online (AOL) is the single most popular Internet Service Provider. America Online combines an easy-to-use interface, an array of resources for AOL subscribers, parental content controls, five e-mail accounts per package, and full Internet access for a reasonable monthly rate. Because of these features and its user-friendly interface AOL remains one of the best ways for beginners to connect to the Internet. America Online can be reached at 800–540–9449 or online (http://www.aol.com).

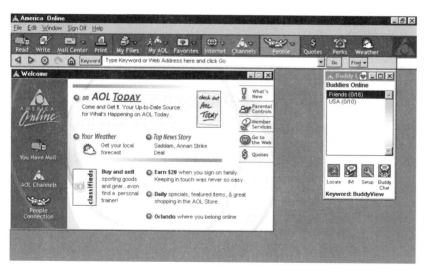

Figure 3: America Online

Local ISPs and national ISPs, such as AT&T WorldNet, are slightly less beginner-friendly than AOL but often compensate with lower costs. Typically such ISPs offer unlimited Internet access for the same or less cost than America Online. However, be aware that local ISPs vary widely. Some have twenty-four-hour free technical support while others have a few college students who answer calls between classes. National ISPs are more consistent but may not be as inexpensive as their local counterparts. Local ISPs can be found in your telephone directory, by word of mouth, or at the Yahoo directory (http://www.yahoo.com). AT&T WorldNet can be contacted at 800-WORLDNET or online (http://www.att.com/worldnet).

An increasingly popular alternative to mainstream ISPs are specialized providers that filter out inappropriate content to make the Internet safer for children. (This is an alternative to similar blocking software reviewed in the next chapter.) One such provider is Rated-G which has local dial-up numbers throughout the country and maintains a list of restricted sites that is updated daily. Rated-G can be reached at 704-544-7071 or on the Web (http://www.rated-g.com).

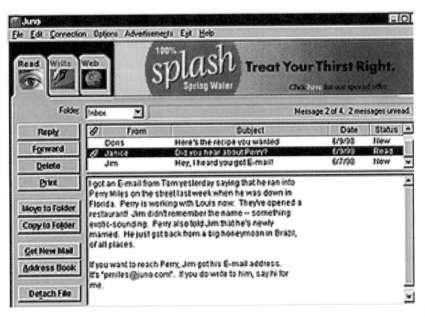

Figure 4: Juno

Finally, for those looking primarily for e-mail access, there's Juno. Juno is a free advertiser-supported e-mail service with local numbers throughout most of the country. Simply install the Juno software on your computer, dial a local number, and you've got free e-mail. Juno does offer Web access as well, but that's not free. Juno is a great way to get your feet wet online, get additional e-mail accounts for family members, or let your child communicate online without the numerous hazards found on the Internet. You can download the software from http://www.juno.com or call 800-654-JUNO to order it.

three
Child-Proofing Your Computer

Computers offer a world of educational opportunities for children, but they aren't child-ready machines by nature. A number of related concerns quickly come to mind (e.g., preventing your son from spilling juice on the keyboard or keeping your daughter from playing with the power cables). Other potential problems, such as ensuring that your computerized address book isn't accidentally erased or protecting your children from Internet pornography, are less evident. Fortunately, there are ways to child-proof your computer and provide for a good learning experience. In this chapter we will discuss some of the concerns, particularly those regarding Internet use, and offer tips and technologies that will help you address them.

Electronic Hazards

There are three broad types of electronic hazards when your child uses the computer: physical risks, data loss, and online dangers.

Physical Risks

The computer is a complex electrical machine and children aren't always the most coordinated. Obviously, the plethora of cables and wires can pose problems for small children. But sometimes the machine is in more danger than the child. For example, if your child spills a drink on the keyboard, he or she won't be electrocuted but you'll probably have to purchase a new keyboard. Therefore, take steps to keep your child and equipment safe.

- Don't allow your child to have food or drink around the computer.
- Make sure all family members wash their hands before using the computer. This not only keeps the keyboard and mouse from getting grimy but will also help prevent the spread of germs.
- Make sure all cables are neatly connected and organized behind the machine.
- Check that all power cables are securely plugged in and there are no exposed plugs or wires.
- Be sure your computer has room for the internal fan to keep the machine cool. The newer processors get very hot, and if the fan exhaust is blocked, you could burn out your machine.
- Keep very young children away from the computer. Despite their attraction to the lights, don't allow them to play with the buttons.

Data Loss

Once the computer is turned on, anyone with access to the machine can wreak havoc upon it. Children are naturally curious, and this interest in the unknown can lead to some nasty results if they accidentally delete critical files. So take steps to prevent such losses.

- Invest in a tape backup system. Backups are the best protection against data loss.

- Install control software such as KidDesk (profiled later in this chapter) and configure each child with appropriate access to computer resources.
- Teach your children which programs on the computer they are, and are not, permitted to run.

Online Dangers

On the one hand, the Internet is perhaps the most significant technology to assist parents with educational computing. On the other hand, there are good reasons to be cautious about letting your children surf the Net. Search engines on the World Wide Web make finding pornography online as easy as typing a few key words. As well as countless personal pages, many established Web sites for pornographic magazines and videos are readily available. Explicit stories, X-rated movie reviews, escort services, and other sordid topics can be found on the Web alongside illegal material such as child pornography. Unfortunately, the relative anonymity of the Internet makes it difficult to track and capture people peddling such material.

If you seek out questionable sites, you'll encounter both pornography and profanity. But obscene sites don't usually jump out at you. In most cases you must intentionally search for them. Online child solicitation, however, is an altogether different concern. Pedophiles take an active role in finding and recruiting children. They may ask for nude photographs from, tell explicit stories to, or request personal meetings with unwitting youngsters. They may even pose as children themselves, attempting to lure minors into personal encounters. Such incidents are most likely to occur on services with instant messages and chat rooms.

The Internet has a unique effect on interpersonal relationships. When people communicate online through electronic mail, discussion groups, or chat sessions, the computer serves as a buffer; you don't actually see each other face-to-face. While there are some advantages to this arrangement, there is also a real danger of false intimacy. The buffer created by the computer often frees people to express themselves in ways they would never do in person. People can expose deep emotions within the protective medium of the Internet and then mistake that openness for real relational intimacy. For instance, a teenager might "fall in love" with someone they've never even seen, or a husband might develop a dangerously personal relationship with a woman he meets in a chat room. This is not to say that friendships can't begin online; they certainly do. But true intimacy requires personal contact and a three-dimensional relationship. The anonymity of the Internet further complicates the situation. As your children (particularly older ones) develop online friendships, be cautiously aware of this dynamic and watch out for relationships that seem to move too quickly.

Information overload and Internet addiction are other subtle dangers of the Internet. Wandering through the Web is analogous to exploring a library—if all of the pages in all of the library books are ripped from their bindings and scattered throughout the building. There are literally millions of Web pages available, and the experience of online exploration can be overwhelming. Some children and adults can't handle the extensive disarray of the Internet. Others are so captivated by the wealth of information and the instantaneous response that they become addicted to it. Both are very real concerns for children against which parents need to guard. Parental preparation, active learning, and planned educational activities help minimize information overload while time limits on Internet usage should help prevent online addiction.

As simplistic as it sounds, commonsense parenting offers the greatest protection for your children. The biggest obstacle to such a plan is the fact that kids often know more about the Internet than their parents. You have taken a major step forward by learning more about the online world. Below are some specific suggestions that will help you protect your family.

- Spend time online without your children. The time that you spend online will not only make you aware of the hazards, but will also encourage your children to explore edifying resources.

- Talk to your children about online dangers. Make them aware of both the good uses and the dangers of the Internet. Clearly establish the boundaries of what is acceptable computer usage.

- Move the computer to an open room. By allowing your kids to hide in a closed room, you make it easier for them to explore the seedy side of the Internet without getting caught. Take the computer out of the den and move it into the family room, where it's harder to be secretive.

- Use parental control features online. Some services, including America Online, allow parents to restrict certain features such as adult material or chat rooms. Take advantage of any of these options.

- Don't give out personal information. By posting your address, phone number, or the name of your child's school, you make it easier for predators to target your children. In the same way, encourage your children not to give such information to strangers.

- Never allow children to arrange phone calls or face-to-face meetings. Since you don't really know who your kids are talking to, such meetings are extremely dangerous.

- Be wary of chat rooms. Whether you choose to block chat room access or to simply monitor time spent in them, be careful. Although they can be a lot of fun, chat rooms can also become hotbeds of obscenities and child solicitation.

- Never reply to offensive or suggestive e-mail messages. Instead, forward them to the system administrator for official action.

- Install Internet filtering software. There are a number of software packages that allow parents to restrict potentially offensive sites. We'll look at some of these in more detail in the next section.

- Finally, if you have reason to believe that your children are in danger, contact appropriate law enforcement officials. The National Center for Missing & Exploited Children and the FBI have established a CyberTipline at 800-843-5678 for calls about Internet-related child sexual exploitation. If your child has been inappropriately approached in a chat room or via e-mail, be sure to report the incident to the CyberTipline.

Computer Control Software

A number of software programs allow parents to control computer use by limiting usage time or by blocking potentially offensive Web sites. Such programs offer some protection when you are not able to supervise your children. But they are not foolproof, so don't be lured into a false sense of security. No blocking program is able to filter 100 percent of the offensive sites. Parental oversight is still essential.

SurfWatch

SurfWatch is strictly an Internet filtering program that contains a database of over a hundred thousand questionable Internet locations. The list includes Web pages, newsgroups, and chat rooms. SurfWatch serves the same purpose as the family-friendly Internet Service Providers mentioned in the previous chapter. But it works with any ISP. Although you cannot supplement this database with your own locations, you can suggest sites to SurfWatch if you feel their database is incomplete. The database is updated daily and can be configured to update automatically while you're online. If you try to visit a restricted site, you'll receive a "Blocked by SurfWatch" message and be denied access.

If you want maximum protection with minimal administrative effort, select SurfWatch. Although it lacks advanced customization, it blocks sites very well and requires little effort to install and maintain. SurfWatch can be purchased by calling 800-458-6600 or visiting their Web site (`http://www.surfwatch.com`).

CrossingGuard

CrossingGuard is a Web filtering program similar to SurfWatch with two noticeable differences—CrossingGuard is produced by a

Christian company and it's free. Crosswalk.com, a popular Christian portal profiled further in chapter 5, has made CrossingGuard freely available for downloading. CrossingGuard does a quality job restricting access to offensive Web sites and virtually all chat rooms (except those sponsored by Christian sites Crosswalk.com and Gospel Communications Network) and requires an approved login before it permits anyone to access the Internet. The program does have some limitations, including running only on Windows systems and not working with America Online. However, it is an excellent basic filtering program sponsored by a company committed to biblical values. To obtain a free copy of CrossingGuard, visit their Web site (http://www.crosswalk.com/crossingguard/).

Cyber Patrol

Cyber Patrol is a general purpose Internet administration program. The password-protected Cyber Patrol Headquarters screen features an hourly calendar for placing time restrictions on Internet usage. As well as restricting or permitting Internet access by making certain hours red or green, you can limit the total number of online hours allowed for a given day or for the whole week. As an added feature, Cyber Patrol can even prevent certain games or applications from being run from your hard drive.

Specific Internet services, including the World Wide Web, newsgroups, and chat rooms can be completely restricted or limited based on content. Cyber Patrol manages a CyberNOT database of pornographic, obscene, and offensive sites. Microsystems Software updates the database weekly based on their research and suggestions from the Internet community. You can personally add sites, even if they aren't obscene, to the CyberNOT list if you don't want your children accessing them. When using the CyberNOT list, if you try to reach a restricted site, you'll see a "Blocked by Cyber Patrol" message across the screen and your attempt will fail. If you prefer a list of prescribed sites, you may use the CyberYES database, which restricts surfing to family-friendly sites specifically cataloged by Microsystems Software. Cyber Patrol also includes ChatGard, which prevents children from divulging personal information (e.g., telephone number or address) while chatting online.

If you are looking for maximum protection and are willing to spend some time configuring the software, then choose Cyber Patrol. Cyber Patrol is available at http://www.cyberpatrol.com or by calling 800-828-2608.

KidDesk Internet Safe

A third product offers features similar to those of SurfWatch and Cyber Patrol but includes complete, powerful, and significantly more user-friendly computer control: KidDesk Internet Safe. KidDesk is actually two programs in one. First, it contains a customizable desktop program where parents can specify exactly which parts of the computer a child will be able to access. Second, it features Internet filtering software to block pornography and other offensive sites. Best of all, KidDesk combines both features in a colorful, child-friendly package.

After you install KidDesk Internet Safe you must configure desktops for each computer user. An automated process helps you create a password-protected account for each person, assign a personalized icon and desktop motif, and add programs for each user to access. (You can even specify which CD-ROMs a user can and cannot run.) This program not only prevents children from using inappropriate software, such as your budget program, but also protects your files from accidental deletion.

You can configure Internet access by first choosing whether to grant access, then restricting surfing to specific pages you have approved or those listed in the KidDesk Kid-Safe Sites directory. You also have the option to regulate chat room access, what information kids can type online, and printing capabilities.

Each user can have his or her own custom desktop with individual access levels, which makes it useful if your children span a wide range of ages. Furthermore, the personalization of the desktop using fun motifs (e.g., pets, sports, or rain forest) makes the computer more kid-friendly.

KidDesk includes a number of built-in, kid-friendly applications including family e-mail, family voice mail, a calendar, name-

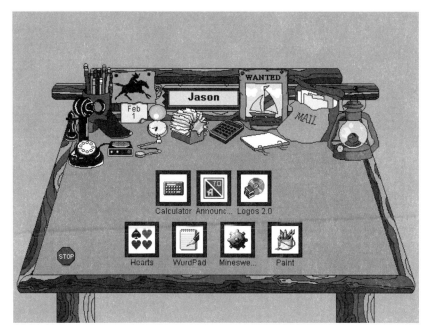

Figure 5: KidDesk

plate, picture frame, and desktop editor that lets children customize the appearance of their desktop. With the e-mail and voice mail capabilities your children can have fun leaving messages to each other and to you without the risks associated with the Internet or the telephone.

KidDesk Internet Safe or KidDesk Family Edition (a scaled down version without the Internet features) are wise additions for any family computer. They are easy to configure, effective at controlling access, and fun for your children. For more information about KidDesk, or to purchase the product, contact Edmark at 800-691-2986 or on the Web (http://www.edmark.com).

General Suggestions

Overall, I have three broad suggestions to help you protect your children and make the most of your computer time. First, be sure that time on the computer (whether online or offline) is part of a planned, active learning event. Like television, computers are flashy and enticing. Therefore they easily become high-tech time wasters. Don't let your child merely sit in front of the computer; plan educational activities. Second, make computer usage a family activity. Spend time together working through a challenging game or exploring the online world. Discover your family's favorite computer activities and demonstrate your own favorites. Finally, limit computer time. Even if you are using a computerized curriculum that demands significant amounts of computer time, be sure you still have lots of non-computer time with your family. Leave the computer room. Take a walk. Go outside. Do things together away from the machine. You'll strengthen your relationships and reinforce the computer's rightful place by doing so.

Remember that you as the parent play the biggest role in determining appropriate use of the computer. Use every technological means necessary to protect your children. But also encourage your children through word and example to follow Paul's admonition from Philippians 4:8: "Finally, brothers, whatever is true, whatever is noble, whatever is right, whatever is pure, whatever is lovely, whatever is admirable—if anything is excellent or praiseworthy—think about such things." Most importantly, pray for your children that their computer use will be educational and to God's glory.

four

Educational Computing

Because many people use their computers only for writing letters, sending e-mail, or playing games, it can be difficult to imagine exactly how computers can be used in education. Let's approach this issue from a number of angles. First we'll look at four educational roles of a computer. Then we'll review five types of educational software and how they can be incorporated into your child's education. Finally, we'll discuss some specific educational activities.

Computer Roles

In his landmark work *The Computer in the School* Robert Taylor defined three basic roles of the computer in education: tutor, tool, and tutee. With the rapid growth of the Internet, experts in the field of instructional technology have added a fourth educational role for the computer: telecommunications device.

Tutor

In the tutor role the software assumes the primary role of instructor, often using tutorials, simulations, and practice drills to educate the student. Computers can serve as effective instructors in areas where parents or teachers lack expertise. If your child wants to learn French, for example, and you speak only English, a tutorial program is an ideal solution. Some homeschooling parents express concern about how to teach children upper-level courses such as calculus, physics, or advanced languages. Quality curriculum programs offer parents the opportunity to continue homeschooling by allowing the computer to teach such advanced subjects. Parents may also decide to work through the computer program either prior to or simultaneously with their child. This approach enables parent and computer to share the role of instructor. In chapter 8 we'll examine computerized curriculum materials such as Alpha Omega's Switched-On Schoolhouse.

Tool

Many teachers prefer to use computers in Taylor's second, most common capacity: as tools. As tools computers don't perform any instruction, but they do serve as an integral part of the lessons. For instance, students may use word processing software to compose English papers, graphic design packages to design greeting cards in art class, or business simulation programs to prepare presentations for an economics lesson. Sometimes you will select computer software specifically designed for a given purpose, such as when you use a genealogy program to map out the lineage of Jesus. However, there is a lot of room for creativity in this area. For example, a spreadsheet progam like Microsoft Excel can be used to help teach mathematics, economics, and even graphing.

Tutee

Taylor's third role, computer as tutee, sounds unusual. In this scenario the student actually teaches the computer. We observe this most often when students learn programming languages such as Visual Basic, Javascript, or C++. Students actually program the computer to perform a function, such as computing compound interest in a bank account. Computers never function solely as tutee, though, because while the computer "learns" from the student, the student also learns about the computer. Programming, in particular, is a great way to teach children about problem solving, structured thinking, and logic. It's also a highly marketable skill in its own right. I've met many students who have found summer jobs creating World Wide Web sites. That not only offers a valuable learning experience but also pays better than the local fast food restaurant! Even if you're not a computer wizard, there are numerous books and tutorials you can use to help a child learn computer programming.

Telecommunications Device

Students and teachers use computers to exchange electronic mail, participate in online discussions, and surf the World Wide Web. The Internet's popularity has prompted many families to purchase computers solely for online use. The president has made it a priority for every school and library to be connected to the Internet. Clearly, the Internet has the potential to be the most significant advance in education since the printing press. It offers countless educational opportunities, ranging from subject-oriented Web sites to detailed online research. We'll examine these in more detail in chapter 5. The Internet has also expanded distance learning opportunities that are particularly helpful for home-schooling parents seeking advanced classes for their children. Accredited online institutions offer programs ranging from associate's to doctoral degrees. Chapter 6 explores these.

These four roles of computers in education serve as a helpful framework for maximizing a computer's use. In fact, I have personal experience with all of them. As I have sought to refresh my Greek skills (which I seem to have forgotten faster than I learned them), I have turned to various computer-based *tutorials*. Through verb charts, vocabulary drills, and translation exercises, the computer has instructed me in Greek. In addition to using Microsoft

Word and Excel for both teaching and learning purposes, I extensively use Bible software as a *tool* for Bible study and lesson preparation. I don't do much software design these days, but I have programmed in a number of computer languages, thus turning my computer into my *tutee*. Finally, the Internet as a *telecommunications device* has been an integral part of my educational experience, especially in my graduate studies. I've taken classes online, interviewed people through e-mail, and searched through article databases while conducting dissertation research. Therefore, I am a firm believer that the computer has a critical place in all four realms.

Educational Roles for Computers

Computer Role	Tutor	Tool	Tutee	Telecommunications Device
Description	Computer as instructor	Computer as assistant	Computer as learner	Computer as communicator
Learning Example	Learning French	Creating a photo montage	Writing an adventure game	Visiting online adventure game
Software Example	Learn to Speak French (The Learning Company)	Photoshop (Adobe)	Visual Basic (Microsoft)	Netscape Navigator (Netscape)

Types of Programs

Educational software can be categorized in various ways. In this book I've divided educational software into five broad categories: tutorial, discovery, edutainment, authoring, and reference. You'll find many other categories in catalogs (e.g., simulation, games, or drill and practice), but I've grouped all of them into the aforementioned five. Let's take a closer look at each of these categories.

Tutorials

Computerized tutorials, the most overtly instructional types of programs, are specifically designed to take the place of a teacher and are fundamentally didactic in nature. Tutorial software comes in a wide variety of styles. Some programs are simply electronic equivalents of textbooks, flashcards, and quizzes. A student might learn to speak a foreign language by running Learn to Speak Spanish in which the computer verbalizes Spanish words for the student, offers electronic chapters on topics such as food-related words, and tests the student on his or her mastery of the language. Other tutorial programs such as Switched-On Schoolhouse incorporate a complete multi-grade, multi-subject electronic curriculum.

Discovery

Discovery programs reverse the learning experience found within tutorials. Rather than the program handing information to the student, the student must take the initiative and begin an electronic journey of exploration. A Walk in the Footsteps of Jesus, a multimedia tour of the Holy Land, lets you wander around Jerusalem, Bethlehem, the Sea of Galilee, and more. While wandering you can literally look around (left, right, up, down) as if you were actually in Israel. Similarly, the A.D.A.M. Nine Month Miracle turns your children into doctors and lets them follow the development of a baby from conception to birth.

Edutainment

Some believe that children will learn better if material is incorporated within a game, so some computer software programs strive to deliver information in a fun context. Edutainment programs combine instruction and entertainment, often taking the form of games that require mastery of particular skills for advancement and victory. Packages such as Math Blaster, where players have to correctly solve math problems to zap space-borne objects, combine arcade-style games with learning drills and provide a fun way for students to learn new information or hone their skills.

Edutainment programs provide reinforcement and practice drills without drudgery for either the teacher or student.

Simulations are an interesting variation on edutainment. Such programs enable students to work through real-life scenarios simulated on the computer. For example, SimCity presents the challenge of designing a city while dealing with politics, finances, crime, employment, and other social factors.

Authoring

Authoring programs permit students to design and develop things such as Web pages, greeting cards, or musical scores. Basic authoring programs include Microsoft Word for word processing and Adobe PageMill for Web development. More targeted applications include advanced graphics editing within Adobe Photoshop and Microsoft Visual Basic or Visual C++ for computer programming. In general, authoring programs provide tools for creating products ranging from memos to architectural designs.

Both broad and focused authoring programs are valuable educational products. Broad authoring products, such as the Microsoft Office suite (word processor, spreadsheet, presentation graphics program, and database), encourage valuable skills that prove useful at all levels of education and in the marketplace. Specialized products, such as graphic design or computer programming, offer students the chance to develop specific skills in their area of interest.

Reference

Finally, reference programs are computerized equivalents of dictionaries, encyclopedias, and other resources you tap into for specific information. With CD-ROMs that hold tens of thousands of written pages on a single disc, it's possible to place an encyclopedia or even an entire library on your home computer. The advantage of computerized reference material is that you can generally perform very fast keyword searches. Programs such as Logos Scholar's Pack enable you to instantly search through multiple Bible translations, commentaries, dictionaries, devotionals, and other reference material. Such programs, combined with the materials on the Internet, make high-quality reference materials available to those who might not otherwise have access to good libraries or resources.

Types of Educational Software

Software Type	Tutorial	Discovery	Edutainment	Authoring	Reference
Purpose	Instruction	Exploration	Make Learning Fun	Creation	Research
Learning Example	Learn fifth grade math, science, history, language arts, and Bible	Visit Jerusalem	Journey on a quest throughout history	Write and direct plays starring the American Girls	Learn about the books of the Bible
Software Example	Switched-On Schoolhouse (Bridgestone Multimedia)	A Walk in the Footsteps of Jesus (Parsons Technology)	Where in Time is Carmen Sandiego (Broderbund)	The American Girls Premiere (The Learning Company)	The Baker Bible Encyclopedia for Kids (Baker Book House/New Kids Media)

Active Learning

The hype surrounding computer education tempts us to believe that parents need only to purchase a computer, install the proper software, and walk away while their children automatically become geniuses. But learning requires work by both instructor and student; learning is an active process.

Even with the best computerized curricula, parents shouldn't relinquish all teaching responsibilities to their computers. There are some things that a computer cannot do. It cannot customize the educational experience to your child's particular learning style.

It cannot read facial expressions to determine when your child is getting lost and when information must be restated. Although it can report that your child incorrectly answered 30 percent of the quiz questions, it cannot explain why. A computer cannot adapt lessons (either in content or style) to the interests, strengths, and weaknesses of the child. It cannot provide the passion that compels a child to learn. Computers cannot encourage children when they apply lessons outside of the classroom. They cannot do any of these things. But parents can. Parents can provide a personal touch the most advanced computer cannot imitate.

Still, there are many things a computer can offer that wouldn't otherwise be possible. Using the Internet, children can gain up-to-the-minute access to newspapers from all over the world. You can watch live footage of major events, medical procedures, or even telescope and satellite images online. Your kids can explore everything from the vast expanse of outer space (in challenging adventure games) to the smallest blood vessel (with a multimedia study of the human body). Computers offer parents, particularly homeschoolers, opportunity to level the playing field with large-budget schools. Your computer allows you to access current information, virtual libraries, and leading teachers.

To make the most of instructional technology, you must purposefully incorporate computer learning experiences into your overall educational plan. For some, the computer may serve simply as a supplement that provides tutoring for specific subjects or reinforcement for challenging topics. Others may decide to purchase a complete computer-based curriculum and coordinate all learning activities around the computer.

The computer will serve different functions for different children, depending on age and temperament. A young child might be captivated by a multimedia storybook of Noah and the ark, but older children will benefit more from watching a surgical procedure online or exchanging e-mail with kids in Europe. While computer use for very young children and software for infants (also called lapware) may not always be worthwhile, there are exceptions. PhonicsTutor, for example, is a great program that helps young children learn to read. As children get older, computers become increasingly more beneficial. For that reason many of the software highlights in chapter 8 are for products targeting children ages seven and above.

For the best overall learning experience, be sure to incorporate other teaching methods such as discussion, reading, experimentation, and exploration. Most children learn best by applying concepts in real-life experiences, so don't neglect offline learning activities. Education shouldn't be limited to formal time, either in front of a computer or in a book. Find out how your child learns best and select software and online activities that complement his or her learning style.

From a biblical perspective, parents are ultimately responsible for their children's education. Parents should view teachers, whether human or computer, as assistants in the educational process. For most families, computers, if properly used, will enhance education. For one family this might mean purchasing a complete CD-ROM curriculum while another family might use the Internet as an electronic library. Regardless, use educational software as part of an *active* learning experience.

Computer Learning Activities

Sometimes it's difficult to come up with specific educational uses for your computer. Chapter 8 will spark some ideas about how to incorporate educational software into your family's learning. To get you started, though, here are a few creative ways to use your computer that will get you thinking about innovative applications for instructional technology.

Grow a Family Tree—Researching your family history can be fun and enlightening for children and parents alike. Use one of the many genealogy programs to help you with your tree, or use the Internet to learn more about your surname.

Build a City—Simulation programs such as SimCity challenge children to design, construct, and maintain a city (or even an entire planet). It's a great way to learn about construction, economics, the environment, and politics—all while having fun.

Visit a Museum—Many of the world's leading museums have produced online or CD-ROM exhibits. Visit a van Gogh, marvel at a Monet, or be dazzled by a da Vinci. As well as providing an opportunity to visit museums you may never physically see, this serves as a good exercise prior to making a real-life visit.

Write an E-pal—Electronic mail really enhances the pen-pal experience. Write to a teacher or homeschooler, perhaps in another country, and arrange for an electronic pen pal for your child. To be safe, don't let your child make these arrangements. Do it yourself. (See chapter 3 for more information about protecting your children online.)

Play the Market—Many investment companies allow you to create a virtual portfolio on their Web site and to follow its progress. Teach your child about investments and the stock market, let them pick out stocks that they like, and follow their progress for awhile. You might even want to set up a contest to see who has the highest return. This exercise will also give you a chance to teach your child about biblical concepts such as stewardship and coveting.

Embark on a Web Hunt—Put together an educational quest where the student must find information online to successfully complete a journey. In addition to improving their research skills, such activities are fun because students find information themselves, often learning other facts along the way.

Read an Interactive Storybook—Multimedia storybooks are becoming increasingly popular. Such programs enable children to read stories themselves, have the computer narrate a story, or simply ask the computer to read selected words or sentences for them. Often a story is loaded with clickable areas that come to life with music or animation when clicked on. It's a new twist on an old favorite.

Learn a New Language—Whether your child wants to learn a foreign language or a programming language, there are countless multimedia tutorials available. You'll find that everything from French and Spanish to Greek and Hebrew to C++ and JavaScript—even American Sign Language—can be learned on the computer.

Produce Animation—A number of design programs enable you to create animated sequences your child can use to create a multimedia storybook of his or her own.

Dissect a Frog—Okay, not everyone has the necessary equipment to dissect a real frog, but anyone can do this on the Web or from a CD-ROM. Walk through the necessary steps and watch the results appear on your computer screen. You may want to use an electronic dissection as a practice run before operating on the real thing.

Learn to Type—Typing is a critical skill in our information age. Numerous typing tutor programs, such as Mavis Beacon and Typing Tutor, are available to help you graduate from hunt-and-peck to touch typing.

Design a Multimedia Timeline—Research a particular period in history. Then, using pictures, sound, and video clips, create a multimedia Web page that presents a timeline of events for the period.

Play a Game—There are some high-quality adventure games, such as Myst and Riven, that will challenge your child's critical thinking and problem-solving skills. Your child will have fun while being challenged in this way. Computerized chess is another favorite—combining an ancient game of thought and skill with modern technology.

Explore the Stars—NASA has developed numerous Web sites with telescope, satellite, and probe imagery. These up-to-the-minute photographs will enhance your study of astronomy.

Plan a Trip—Extensive geographical information is available on the Internet. From city home pages to detailed roadmaps, you'll find everything you need to plan a trip. Get your child involved in the planning process and they'll be more excited for the journey.

Read Local, National, and International Newspapers—Many newspapers have hit the Web with electronic versions of their printed editions. Such electronic papers present numerous research possibilities, comparisons of major stories and editorial slants, and an opportunity to learn about many different cultures.

Record Music—Any computer with a soundcard, speakers, and a microphone is practically a digital recording studio. Even with inexpensive editing software, such as PowerTracks Pro or Digital Orchestrator, you can record, edit, and mix music.

Listen to Online Radio—Using RealAudio you can tune in to numerous radio stations and broadcasts from around the world. Not only can you find entertainment in this way, you can also listen to educational shows not carried by your local stations.

Study the Bible—Many excellent Bible study programs are available for both kids and adults. Some will even help you prepare Bible study lessons for your children or allow them to prepare lessons for you to study. What better way to use your computer than by studying the most important book ever written?

Explore the World—Programs such as A Walk in the Footsteps of Jesus and the Trail Adventure Collection put you in the middle of a distant (either by geography or time) land and let you experience the sights.

Master Math—If math is a frustrating subject for your child, try one of the numerous math programs available to help kids overcome math phobia. They actually make learning fun.

Create a Newsletter—Desktop publishing packages (or even high-end word processors) make it possible for anyone to publish a newsletter, newspaper, or book. Gather a group of children and publish a monthly newspaper. The children will learn while writing articles, taking and scanning photographs, creating and selecting graphics, and laying out the publication. And they'll be excited to share their creation with others.

Take a Class—The Internet features numerous classes, ranging from self-paced tutorials to group distance learning, on a wide variety of topics. From financial investing and computer programming to philosophy and science, there are plenty of classes to satisfy children and adults.

By combining a variety of educational software programs and online activities, your computer can be an integral part of the learning experience. For instance, develop a science scavenger hunt that incorporates both online and offline searching. Incorporate computer software into a traditional lesson. Engage in a Palm Sunday Bible study where you use A Walk in the Footsteps of Jesus to visually show your children the road where the triumphal entry took place. Study Lincoln's Gettysburg Address and then use Writing Blaster to create a multi-panel storyboard of the event. Such hybrid activities are excellent uses of your computer. They allow software to be used as reinforcement for your children—letting them learn a skill and then test their abilities.

The Key to Successful Educational Computing

Preparation is the key to successful educational computing. As a parent or teacher, you need to take time to prepare active learning experiences for your child. This may mean you will need to do some learning on your own, so you know how to harness the computer with your child. You should always evaluate activities upon completion and determine how experiences can be improved for future learning activities. Recent studies have revealed that much of the educational computer use in schools has been largely ineffective because teachers haven't used it well. Simply placing a child in front of a computer to perform endless electronic drills isn't effective instruction. But when teachers plan active learning experiences, results are impressive. Planning and evaluation are perhaps the most difficult and time-consuming parts of the learning process—teaching is a high biblical calling that requires a lot of effort. Its rewards, however, are well worth the labor.

five

Online Educational Resources

Because of the millions of Web pages available, it's often overwhelming trying to sort the wheat from the chaff. Therefore, this chapter offers a selection of quality Web sites culled from countless hours of Web surfing. You will find online directories to help you navigate the Web on your own as well as Christian and general educational sites.

Internet Directories

Although the Internet lacks a master directory, there are numerous topical listings and search features that will help you find information online. The following Web sites, listed alphabetically, represent the leading directories currently available:

- *AltaVista* (http://www.altavista.com)—A powerful searching tool that enables both simple and complex queries. Features an option to limit results to family-friendly sites.

- *AOL NetFind* (http://www.aol.com/netfind/)—A directory and searching tool sponsored by America Online. Features a kids-only search.
- *CrossSearch* (http://www.crosssearch.com)—A Christian Web directory sponsored by Gospel Communications Network.

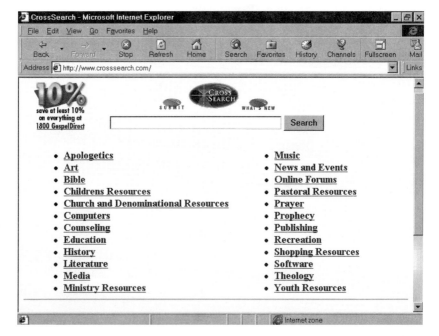

Figure 6: CrossSearch

- *Deja.com* (http://www.deja.com)—Browse or search an archive of topical discussion board postings. You can also post messages through DejaNews.
- *Disney's Internet Guide* (http://www.dig.com)—A directory of Web resources created especially for children. Features periodic tours of thematic Web sites.
- *Education World* (http://www.education-world.com)—A directory and search engine for over 100,000 education-oriented Web sites. Also features articles, reviews, and message boards.

- *Goshen* (http://www.goshen.net)—A Christian Web directory sponsored by Media Management. Also features an online study library, Christian shareware, and message boards.
- *Yahoo* (http://www.yahoo.com)—The most popular Internet subject directory of the Web.
- *Yahooligans* (http://www.yahooligans.com)—A kids-only version of the Yahoo directory.

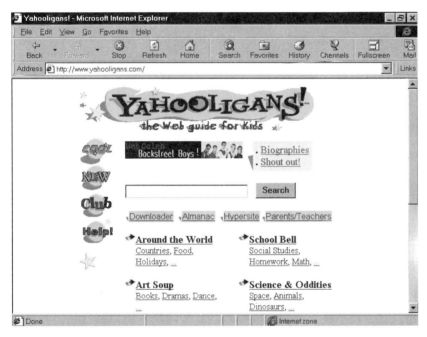

Figure 7: Yahooligans

Christian Educational Resources

The Christian community has done a fine job of harnessing the Internet for the building of God's kingdom. Here are some quality Christian educational Web sites for your learning pleasure:

- *All About Jesus* (http://www.geocities.com/~perkin shome/children.html)—Bible studies for kids ages preschool through twelve, games, puzzles, activity pages, holiday features, and a newsletter for kids.

- *Beantown* (http://www.calvary.com/beantown)—Calvary Chapel Monterey Bay sponsors this Web site containing Bible stories, puzzles, crafts, recipes, science experiments, and fun facts.

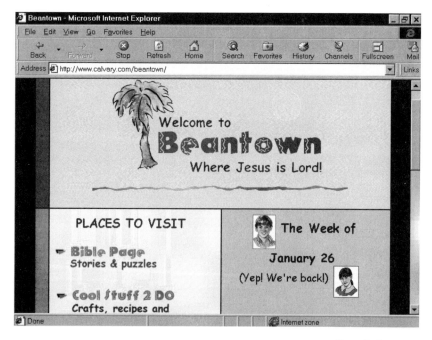

Figure 8: Beantown

- *Bible Gateway* (http://www.gospelcom.net/bible/)—Read or search multiple English translations of the Bible plus German, French, Latin, Spanish, and others.
- *Boundless Webzine* (http://www.boundless.org)—An online magazine for college students, written from a Christian perspective and publised by Focus on the Family.
- *Campus Journal* (http://www.cj.org/)—Features a daily devotional for students of all ages.

- *The Children's Chapel* (http://www.misslink.org/children/)—Read more than fifty Bible stories with matching memory verse, prayer, and contemporary story.
- *Children's Sonshine Network* (http://www.kidsradio.org)—Listen to children's radio broadcasts on the Web. Features *Adventures in Odyssey, Keys for Kids, Kids' Talk, Nutty News,* and more.
- *Christian Classics Ethereal Library* (http://www.ccel.wheaton.edu)—Classic Christian writings that can be read online, downloaded to your computer, or printed. CCEL includes writings from Augustine, Chambers, Chesterton, Edwards, Spurgeon, Wesley, and others—all available at no cost.
- *Crosswalk.com* (http://www.crosswalk.com)—A Christian portal featuring sections on homeschooling, music, money, movies, and more. In addition to articles, streaming audio, and chat areas, Crosswalk.com offers CrossingGuard, an Internet filtering solution profiled in chapter 3.
- *Eclectic Homeschool Online* (http://www.eho.org/)—An online magazine, written by and for homeschoolers, that features creative learning ideas, reviews of educational materials, and general information for homeschooling families.
- *Focus on the Family* (http://www.family.org)—A wealth of online resources including radio broadcasts of *Focus on the Family* and *Adventures in Odyssey* delivered through streaming audio, articles, movie and television reviews.
- *Home School Legal Defense Association* (http://www.hslda.org)—A wealth of information for homeschoolers including legal tips, a resource library, current events in homeschooling, and an online tutorial on constitutional law.
- *Into the Wardrobe: The C. S. Lewis Web Site* (http://cslewis.drzeus.net)—For Narnia fans, this Web site provides an extensive introduction to C. S. Lewis and his writings.
- *Kids' Quest* (http://www.christiananswers.net/kids/)—Activities, stories, audio, video, answers to kids' questions, and more delivered in an online rain forest set-

ting. This site by the Christian Answers Network is an educational resource that helps kids learn about the Creator by exploring his creation.

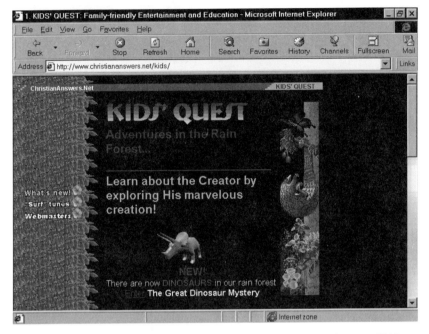

Figure 9: Kids' Quest

- *Kidzweb* (http://www.kidzweb.org)—Learn practical applications of biblical principles through humorous comics, ask questions about the Bible, and subscribe to a kids' e-mail newsletter.
- *NetCentral* (http://www.netcentral.net)—Christian music galore—listen to music, browse artist Web sites, read articles and reviews, join in online discussions, and more.
- *Online Discover Bible Guides* (http://www.iiw.org/discover/)—Online guides that help you explore major themes in the Bible such as eternal life, heaven, prayer, and suffering.
- *WWJD* (http://www.wwjd.com)—A site helping teens learn to answer the question, "What would Jesus do?" Features

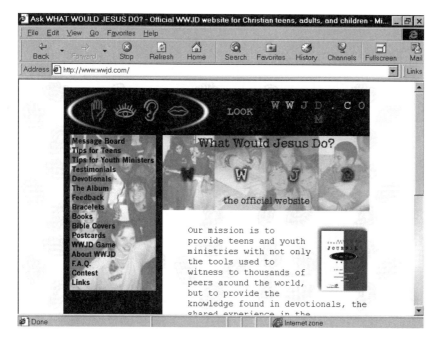

Figure 10: WWJD

devotionals, testimonials, postcards, message boards, and a game.

General Educational Resources

The Web offers a combination library, museum, and laboratory at your fingertips. The following educational Web sites are excellent resources for the whole family.

- *Adventures from The Book of Virtues* (http://www.pbs.org/adventures/)—Animated adventures based on William Bennett's excellent collection of stories. Read virtuous stories, play games, or print coloring pages.
- *America's Health Network* (http://www.ahn.com/)—In addition to an excellent repository of health and medical information, this site features multimedia explorations of vari-

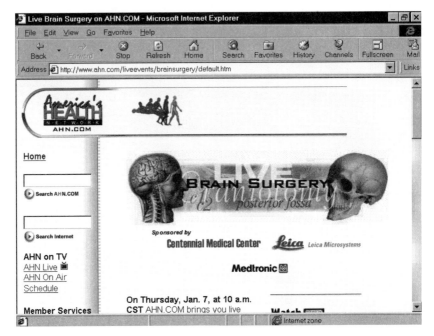

Figure 11: America's Health Network

ous topics including the heart, eyes, knee, and hair. Furthermore, the site contains live and archived video presentations of medical procedures including brain, eye, and open heart surgery and a section called "Self-Management of Symptoms" which offers counsel for helping sick kids and adults.

- *Ask Dr. Math* (http://forum.swarthmore.edu/dr.math/)—Do you want to know how to add large numbers, multiply negative numbers, understand prime numbers, or raise things to powers? Ask Dr. Math. This site features math questions and answers from children and their parents as well as weekly math challenges for students of all ages.

- *Biographical Dictionary* (http://www.s9.com/biography/)—Search through brief biographical sketches of more than twenty-five thousand people.

Figure 12: Bonus.com

- *Bonus.com* (http://bonus.com/)—A Web site with games, explorations, learning activities, experiments, and a lot more in a kids-oriented environment.
- *Bradford Robotic Telescope Observatory* (http://www.tele scope.org/rti/)—You can send observation requests to this fully robotic telescope and retrieve images the next day. The site also features information about the workings of the telescope, an introduction to stars and galaxies, and weather reports.
- *Children's Television Workshop* (http://www.ctw.org)—From the Sesame Street gang comes this Web site full of activities for children, including family Web activities, preschool games and stories, a tool to help kids build their own Web page, and, of course, lots of information about the famous muppets.
- *Classroom Connect Quests* (http://quest.classroom.com)— Classroom Connect sends a group of explorers on a quest

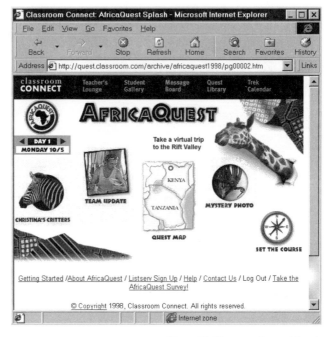

Figure 13: Classroom Connect Quests

and then enables students to participate in the journey through regularly updated pictures, maps, journals, and discussion sessions with other students and the explorers themselves. Recent quests include the Galapagos Archipelago, Africa's Great Rift Valley, and the Mayan rain forest.

- *Complete Works of Shakespeare* (http://www.tech.mit.edu/shakespeare/works.html)—Read all of Shakespeare's works, complete with a hypertext glossary of significant words. Also features familiar quotations from the Bard.

- *Crayola* (http://www.crayola.com)—Although this Web site is ultimately designed as a promotion for Crayola, it offers an excellent children's area featuring weekly stories, artwork, crafts, coloring pages, and a tour of the crayon factory.

- *dMarie Time Capsule* (http://www.dmarie.com/asp/history.asp)—Enter any date since 1900 and learn what was happening in the world—birthdays, headlines, popular songs, and the cost of everyday items are included in the time capsule summary.

- *Evidence: The True Witness* (http://library.advanced.org/17049/)—Learn about forensics—the science that examines evidence in criminal cases and legal matters. Read up on a variety of forensic science topics including DNA structures, fingerprinting, and pathology. Assume the role of an ace detective and try your sleuthing skills at solving a complex mystery.

- *Exploration in Education* (http://www.stsci.edu/exined/)— Features electronic tutorials, reports, and picture books about current astronomy and planetary research. Topics include Jupiter, Orion, Mars, and images from the Hubble Space Telescope.

- *For Young Writers* (http://www.inkspot.com/joe/young/)—Articles, tips, links, and message boards for young writers. Learn how to improve your writing and where you can publish your work.

- *Free Online Unit Studies* (http://www.alaska.net/~cccandc/free.htm)—Over two hundred online unit studies available at no cost. Topics include cells and systems, China, the Civil War, mammals, Mexico, money, transportation, Valentine's Day, and more.

- *FunBrain* (http://www.funbrain.com/)—FunBrain features online games and exercises, grouped by age, that cover a variety of topics including spelling, grammar, math, music, and geography. For parents and teachers, FunBrain enables you to create online quizzes for your students to take and automatically e-mails the results to you.

- *The Gateway* (http://www.thegateway.org/)—An extensive directory of lesson plans, curriculum units, and other educational materials to assist parents and teachers. Sponsored by the U.S. Department of Education.

- *How Stuff Works* (http://www.howstuffworks.com)—Learn about everything from cars, airplanes, and microwave ovens

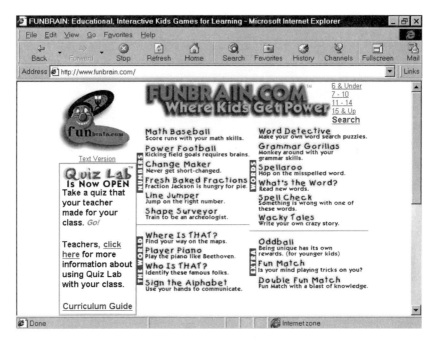

Figure 14: FunBrain

to televisions, stock markets, and sunburns. Every week a new article is added to teach you how stuff works.

- *HyperHistory Online* (http://www.hyperhistory.com)—An integrated world history chart featuring linked timelines, events, maps, and people. Entries are color-coded to identify their cultural and historical context.

- *Little Explorers* (http://www.enchantedlearning.com/Dictionary.html)—An online picture dictionary for young ones. Click on a letter and a picture index for words that begin with that letter appears, complete with links to corresponding Web pages.

- *Mega Mathematics* (http://www.c3.lanl.gov/mega-math/)—A Web site dedicated to making math interesting and fun. Read stories, view pictures, play some math games, and learn how math affects so many aspects of life.

- *Microsoft TerraServer* (http://www.terraserver.micro soft.com)—Explore the world using aerial photographs and satellite imagery. You can start with a map of the world and zoom in close enough to see your own neighborhood.
- *My Virtual Reference Desk* (http://www.refdesk.com/)—The latest news (print and audio), quotations, maps, encyclopedia, thesaurus, dictionary, fact book, yellow pages, and more.
- *National Archives Online Exhibit Hall* (http://www.nara .gov/exhall/exhibits.html)—Historical exhibits from the National Archives and Records Administration. View images of historic documents such as the Declaration of Independence and the Constitution, panoramic photographs from the World War I era, presidential gifts and speech cards, and other American historical events.
- *The National Gallery of Art* (http://www.nga.gov/)—Browse an ever-expanding online collection of fine art. Many presentations parallel the actual exhibits at the National Gallery.
- *The New York Times Learning Network* (http://www.nytimes .com/learning/)—Current events, historical accounts, lesson plans, quizzes, puzzles, and discussion with newspaper reporters—all sponsored by the *New York Times*.
- *Online Children's Stories* (http://www.acs.ucalgary.ca/ ~dkbrown/stories.html)—Read, download, or print numerous children's stories ranging from classics such as *Little Women* and *The Jungle Book* to nursery rhymes, poems, and folklore.
- *OnlineClass* (http://www.onlineclass.com)—OnlineClass offers short courses (approximately eight weeks) that can be used to supplement studies. Recent topics include Antarctica, ocean explorers, the ferris wheel, and urban architecture.
- *Piano on the Net* (http://www.artdsm.com/music.html)— Yes, you can learn how to play the piano with a series of online lessons. Of course, it helps to have a piano handy.
- *Project Gutenberg* (http://www.promo.net/pg/)—This is the secular equivalent of the aforementioned Christian Classics

Ethereal Library. Project Gutenberg contains over fifteen hundred books (including light literature, heavy literature, and reference works) freely available for reading or printing.

- *Quest: NASA K–12 Internet Initiative* (`http://quest.arc.nasa.gov`)—Features live chats with NASA space scientists, live and archived events including launches and tours, testing of a replica of the Wright brothers' plane, and other air- and space-oriented activities.

- *Smithsonian Magazine's Kids' Castle* (`http://www.kidscastle.si.edu/`)—Kids' Castle features articles and photos on sports, history, the arts, travel, science, and air and space. The site also features games, contests, and message boards.

- *Teachnet* (`http://www.teachnet.com`)—Lesson plans, activity suggestions, and other information to help parents and teachers creatively educate children.

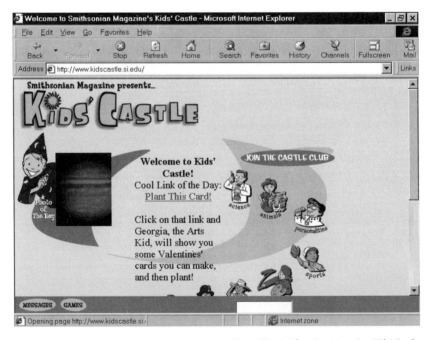

Figure 15: Smithsonian Magazine Kids' Castle

- *Virtual Frog Dissection Kit* (`http://www.itg.lbl.gov/vfrog/`)—Dissect a frog on the Web. With text, graphics, photographs, and video clips you can learn all about frogs.

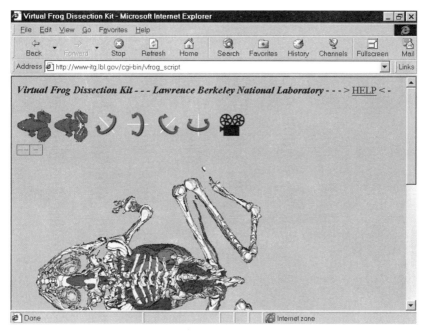

Figure 16: Virtual Frog Dissection Kit

- *The White House for Kids* (`http://www.whitehouse.gov/WH/kids/html/kidshome.html`)—Information about the White House, government, and American history, written for children. Also features links to the main White House site, which contains a virtual library, information about the federal government, and current news out of Washington, D.C.
- *Zoom* (`http://www.pbs.org/wgbh/zoom/`)—Affiliated with the PBS show of the same name, this Web site is created by kids, for kids, and about kids. Features crafts, games, reviews, ideas, chat, and other kid stuff.

six

Christian
Distance Education

Distance education is one of the hottest topics in educational technology today. It's not a new phenomenon. Some believe that Paul's circular letters were the first example of distance education. In modern times distance education began with the first correspondence courses offered over a hundred years ago. But educational possibilities created by the Internet and World Wide Web have moved the issue into the mainstream. Distance education opens doors to parents, homeschoolers, and adults interested in furthering their education. Not only can you take individual classes for personal enrichment or to supplement a curriculum, but you can find accredited distance education programs from kindergarten through Ph.D studies. In this chapter we'll describe distance education, look at its benefits, discuss the accreditation issue, and highlight some of the programs currently available.

The New Face of Distance Education

At one time the only type of distance education was independent study. Today this is still a form of distance education, but it's not the only form. Today's distance classes have a much higher level of interaction, not only between student and instructor but also among fellow students within a class. Many distance learning courses consist of groups of students who interact over the Internet via e-mail, discussion groups, chat rooms, and Web pages, or by means of conference calls and videoconference. Programs often feature some type of residency where you spend a few weeks on-campus with your classmates. Other nontraditional forms of education often grouped with distance education include mentoring, portfolio development, challenge examinations, classes that meet at satellite campuses, cluster groups, and modular class sessions.

Independent studies are pretty self-explanatory. When you register for a course, you receive various materials, such as audio- or videotaped lectures, course outlines, books, and assignment listings. Within a specified time limit, you are required to work through all of the course material and complete the various assignments. Often independent study assignments are written projects, though some programs do include proctored exams, which are then sent to a faculty member for grading. Generally you submit assignments as you go along so you can receive feedback on your work. When you've completed all of the assignments to the instructor's satisfaction, you receive a final grade for the course.

Interactive learning using the Internet has transformed traditional distance education. Unlike traditional independent studies, online distance learning allows multiple students to participate in a class together and to interact with each other and the instructor. Like traditional classes, such distance learning classes run on a quarter or semester schedule. Rather than marking time by lecture dates, however, the semester is typically divided into weeks. Each week you, the student, receive lecture material—on videotape, audiotape, or World Wide Web—which is typically supplemented by assigned reading. Then you have weekly assignments, ranging from brief essays to large projects, that you must complete and submit to your instructor, often via e-mail. At the same time, you can participate in class discussions online with your fellow students. Because such discussions often use message boards, students don't all have to be online simultaneously. Rather, you post your message at a time convenient to you, and others read and respond to it when they are online. You may actually have some pretty interesting class discussions this way, and you'll have an archive of them throughout the semester.

Parents have found diverse ways to harness distance education. Some use diploma or degree programs as the primary educational framework for homeschooling. Others enroll their children in individual classes to supplement education. Gifted and special needs students are able to take college courses, or even earn whole degrees, while still at home. Finally, parents themselves can take advantage of distance degree programs to earn bachelor's or graduate degrees—something that wouldn't be possible, either geographically or logistically, through traditional means. As someone who has both taken and taught courses at a distance, I'm a major advocate of distance education.

Benefits of Distance Education

Distance education students enjoy the significant benefit of flexibility. Distance education allows parents to supplement a child's learning experience with subjects that might be beyond their realm of expertise. For example, if your daughter wants to take trigonometry but math was never your strong point, she could enroll in a distance learning math class. Distance classes can be either high-tech independent studies or a group class with a fixed schedule. You can choose the option that fits your circumstances and learning style. Distance education enables adults to take classes or work on a degree without sacrificing job or family commitments. Such classes also benefit those who need immediate training and those who would learn better without the rigid structure of a traditional program.

It might be hard to believe (especially for those of us who teach for a living), but students learn through distance education as well as or better than they do in traditional classrooms. Homeschoolers and others involved in nontraditional educational endeavors have already learned that the traditional one-size-fits-all classroom isn't always the best solution. It's important to know how you learn best and then to select an educational approach that works for you. For instance, if you find that you prefer audio-based instruction, then you probably shouldn't pick a class (either traditional or distance) that relies on books and articles for primary instruction. If you have difficulty sitting through a three-hour graduate class, you would be better served by a distance class where you can absorb material at scattered times throughout the week. There are many choices; find something that works for you and go with it.

Accreditation

Accreditation is a voluntary process by which primary and secondary schools, colleges, universities, and professional schools submit themselves to a comprehensive review process by an outside agency that ensures quality and institutional integrity. Accreditation is the leading indicator that an institution is running a quality educational program.

The most credible type of accreditation in the United States is called regional accreditation, which means that an institution is accredited by one of the six geographically dispersed associations approved by the U.S. Department of Education:

Middle States Association of Colleges and Schools
New England Association of Schools and Colleges
North Central Association of Colleges and Schools
Northwest Association of Schools and Colleges
Southern Association of Colleges and Schools
Western Association of Schools and Colleges

Each of these regional accrediting agencies has a commission designated specifically for primary and secondary schools and higher education institutions. The recent growth in distance education has challenged accrediting agencies, but they have taken steps to address the new issues. To address the needs of distance education offerings by primary and secondary schools, the regional accrediting agencies have created a new accrediting agency called the Commission on International and Transregional Accreditation (CITA). The higher education commissions have continued to work within the existing regional structure to address such issues.

Accreditation is essential when seeking a post-secondary school because most universities, employers, and financial aid programs will not recognize unaccredited degrees. Because of the relative newness of CITA and the other regulations that govern K–12 home education efforts, however, such accreditation is less critical when evaluating K–12 distance programs. There are even some quality Christian schools that don't seek regional accreditation for theological reasons. Despite these exceptions, however, accreditation remains the standard of quality within the United States. So I strongly advise that you consider accreditation when seeking a distance education program. This will not only guarantee a quality program but will also ensure that other schools or employers will not question your efforts.

Program Highlights

Since there are distance education options available for all ages, let's look at a few quality programs that cover the spectrum from individual courses to complete diploma and degree programs. Students can take individual classes from most of these programs without enrolling for an entire diploma or degree.

- *The Calvert School Home Instruction Department* (410-243-6030, http://www.calvertschool.org)—The Calvert School program, which offers a complete home instruction curriculum for children ages kindergarten through eighth grade, was the first such program to receive CITA accreditation. Courses are drawn from Calvert's Day School curriculum and participating students have regular contact with Day School teachers.

- *University of Nebraska-Lincoln Department of Distance Education* (402-472-4321, http://www.unl.edu/conted/disted/)— The University of Nebraska-Lincoln offers a complete, North Central accredited, high school curriculum through distance education. Historically the program has been a traditional independent study but UNL is currently developing an interactive online program as well.

- *HomeSat* (800-739-8199, http://www.homesat.com)—The Home Satellite Network offers a Christian K–12 program through satellite or videotape-based distance learning. Home-Sat is affiliated with Bob Jones University and uses the popular BJU Press Christian homeschooling curriculum. Bob Jones University will not seek accreditation for theological reasons, but their programs on all levels are excellent.

- *Liberty University* (800-424-9595, http://www.liberty.edu/Admissions/)—This accredited Christian university offers a number of bachelor's degrees through distance learning. Students can earn a 120-credit Bachelor of Science degree in business (with specializations in accounting, management, finance, or marketing), psychology, religion, or multidisciplinary studies. Liberty also offers master's degrees in religion, divinity, and counseling.

- *Jones International University* (800-811-5663, http://www.jonesinternational.edu)—Jones International University (JIU) is the first regionally accredited virtual university—all of the courses and degrees offered through JIU are delivered entirely through the Internet. There are no buildings, chalkboards, or any travel associated with JIU programs. JIU offers a B.A. completion degree for those with sixty or more credits, an M.A. degree in business communication, and numerous certificate programs. Students can also register for individual classes that begin every four weeks.

- *Regent University* (800-373-5504, http://www.regent.edu/distance/)—Regent is an accredited graduate-only Christian university that has multiple master's degrees available via distance education. Students can earn graduate degrees in business, communication, divinity, education, government, organizational leadership, and law. Regent also offers online Ph.D. programs in communication and organizational leadership.
- *Nova Southeastern University* (800-541-6682, http://www.nova.edu/cwis/disted/)—Nova Southeastern has been a leader in accredited distance education for many years and has multiple limited residency doctoral programs available. Students can earn a Ph.D. in computer science, computer information systems, computing technology in education, information systems, information science, or dispute resolution. Nova also offers Ed.D. programs in child and youth studies or instructional technology and distance education as well as numerous master's degree programs.

These are but a sampling of the growing number of distance education programs available. Since most distance institutions maintain Web pages, the Internet is a great resource to find additional information about other programs. However, be aware that the Internet has also fostered the rise of many degree mills and other questionable programs. To be safe, stick with regionally accredited programs. For a listing of accredited Christian higher education programs available through distance education, visit my Center for Christian Distance Education Web site (http://www.ccde.org).

seven

Selecting Educational Software

I often get e-mail from parents who have recently purchased a computer and are looking for quality educational software programs to get for their kids. Unlike games and productivity packages, there are few educational software packages with high name recognition. Many early educational programs were either low-grade video games with questions tossed in or simply computerized books that required keystrokes to turn pages. Fortunately the field has improved over the years, and it continues to grow as companies strive to produce better programs. A number of companies are even producing Christian educational software geared for both children and adults. Let's look at some of the issues you should consider before running to your local computer store to make a purchase.

Making a Selection

Especially since we're dealing with children, selecting educational software is probably more art than science. While one child may be enamored with a program you choose, another may toss it aside after only one use. However, there are some questions you can ask when considering software that might improve your odds.

Is it compatible with your computer? It's heartbreaking for both child and parent when a gift won't run on the family computer. Confirm that the program will run on your operating system (Windows 98, Macintosh System 8, etc.) and that your computer has enough memory (both RAM and hard drive space) to support it. Be aware that some newer software packages are designed for recent multimedia machines and require components such as a CD-ROM, sound card, and speakers.

Is it compatible with your child's interests and abilities? This may be a more difficult task than matching the program to your computer because your child's interests and abilities constantly change. Make sure that the program is targeted for your child's age group and that the content matches his or her interests. Ask your child if he or she has ever used the program before or if it sounds interesting. Talk to other parents or teachers to find out whether they've used the program in a similar situation, and find out which other programs they recommend.

Is it sufficiently educational? Some companies insert a minimal amount of educational activity into a computer game and then label it edutainment. Research the product you're considering, making sure it has enough educational material to be worthwhile.

Is it compatible with your child's learning styles? As a parent, you probably know better than anyone else how your child learns. If she is an audio learner, then select software that makes extensive use of speech and sound. If he is more visual, make sure the software has rich graphics and uses them well. Match the software to your child. Remember, what works best for one child may not be the most appropriate for another.

Is it recent? Many discount stores offer cut-rate CD-ROM software, such as a reading tutor for under ten dollars, simply distributed in the CD case without any documentation. Generally, this software is either of a lower quality than competing programs or it's old. With few exceptions (e.g., SimCity Classic), software from the DOS era is simply inferior to more recent programs. Many quality programs from a few years ago have been updated with recent versions that offer many more features than their original releases. Therefore, I encourage you to spend your money wisely and stick to current releases.

Is it adaptable? Does the program adapt itself to the level of the student or does it at least have a variety of knowledge levels to choose from? As with clothing, one size fits all rarely works as well as advertised. Ideally the program should adjust questions, examples, or level of difficulty based on the student's performance and allow the student to save profile information for future use. Minimally the program should offer students (or parent/teacher) the option of selecting a skill level.

Is it kid-friendly? Let's face it, if software bores your child it's not going to get used. Is the program full of colorful graphics, sounds, and other novelties that will keep a child's attention? Does the program encourage the child when he or she is successful and assist him or her with struggles? Is it easy enough to use without having to read directions? Program control is also an important factor to consider. Can the child skip over opening credits and pauses quickly? Can they easily move forward and backward through the program?

Is it well supported? Can you call the company with technical questions if you run into trouble? If the program doesn't work well (or at all) on your machine, can you return it? Answering these questions up front will save you many headaches.

In addition to these questions, consider the following purchasing strategies. First, look for an opportunity to try a program before you purchase it. Many public libraries have computers and educational software you can use during your visit. Others permit you to check out CD-ROMs and try products at home. If your church has a media center or you are part of a homeschooling co-op, suggest building an educational software library. Giving parents opportunity to test-drive software before purchase or to borrow products for limited use would prove a valuable service. Sharing your experiences with other parents and seeking their input is also wise. As well as learning about which products to purchase (and which to avoid) you can swap creative computer uses.

Testing Your Choice—Shareware

Shareware is copyrighted software that is available for interested users to test on a "try-before-you-buy" plan. Consumers can download shareware freely off the Internet or purchase a CD-ROM containing dozens of shareware programs for a nominal cost. Typically shareware programs are fully functional but expire after a trial period. After testing shareware for a set time period, you must either purchase a license or delete the program from your computer. Ideally, shareware is a win-win situation for both the author and user. The software author gets wide distribution of a product for a minimal marketing investment, while the user gets the opportunity to test-drive software before making a purchase. For those of us who lament the often high cost of software, shareware is a great idea.

Unfortunately many shareware applications, particularly educational and Christian software products, have not kept up with advancing technology. There was a time that there was a high-quality, low-cost shareware alternative for most major commercial products. However, this is no longer the case, and many shareware programs are clearly inferior to their commercial counterparts. This is not to say that all of them are. A number of shareware Bible software programs, such as The Online Bible, Sword-Searcher, and Theophilos, are excellent.

Because of the popularity of the Internet and the success of the shareware concept, many companies have made demo or abbreviated versions of their products available online. This is a great way to test a commercial product before purchasing it, and it serves as a nice compromise between shareware and commercial software. Often such demos can be found at the software publisher's Web site or at shareware libraries such as Shareware.com (http://www.shareware.com) or the Goshen Christian Shareware Library (http://www.christianshareware.net).

Final Tips

Before you make any software purchase, it's important to con-sider how you will use the software you purchase. For example, you must think deliberately about how you plan to use software in your child's educational experience. Otherwise, your computer may devolve into as much of a mindless time-waster as the tele-vision. As with television viewing, there is a difference between quality learning opportunities and wasting time in front of the screen. Make sure your selections promote quality time.

Don't look solely to others for your usage strategy either. It's easy to make purchases based on how others have successfully used a particular product, and then end up leaving it on your bookcase because it wasn't the right software for your child. So again, consider how *you* will use the software before buying it.

eight
Educational Software Highlights

The number of educational software programs available, both Christian and general, is simply overwhelming. Rather than providing an endless catalog of such products, I will highlight only those that are exceptionally worthwhile. First, I'll spotlight three exceptionally impressive programs, then we'll look at a variety of packages grouped by the five categories listed in chapter 4. These programs cover a wide range of topics and ages, but all are quality programs that would make good additions to any educational software library.

Software in the Spotlight

Three Christian programs, ranging in age from elementary through graduate school, deserve particular recognition for their exemplary status. Not only are these must-have programs, but they also set the standard for Christian educational software.

Bibleland.com

```
Ages: 7-12
Operating System: Windows or Macintosh
Baker Book House
800-877-2665
http://www.bakerbooks.com
```

Bibleland.com harnesses the World Wide Web's popularity and ease of navigation to present a highly creative introduction to the Bible. If you can imagine the Web being around during biblical times (meaning that most people would have their own Web pages), then you begin to picture this program. Bibleland.com simulates a Web browser that allows you to surf the personal home pages of key biblical figures. Sites with addresses such as www.Adam.com introduce you to over a hundred people ranging from the popular (David, Jonah, Moses, and Noah) to the lesser known (Boaz, Jethro, Rahab, and Zerubbabel). Each Web page reflects the character's perspective and includes graphics, frequently asked questions, audio and video clips, and links to other resources. Most Web pages contain links directly to the biblical text, in the kid-friendly New Living Translation, which children can read themselves or request that the computer read for them. The *Baker Bible Dictionary for Kids* is also incorporated into the program so children can click on highlighted words and read the associated definition.

To increase curiosity and learning opportunities, the program sends children e-mail messages leading them to certain Web pages. Clicking on the e-mail box might reveal a message from Carlie that reads, "In the days before overnight express mail, a very important message is delivered by a disembodied hand" with a link to www.Belshazzar. When you click on the link, you are taken to The Most Excellent Home Page of Belshazzar, Most Excellent King of Babylon.

This program is engaging, educational, and just plain fun; it's an excellent example of multimedia educational software making learning enjoyable. If you've got younger children, be sure to add this one to your collection.

Figure 17: Bibleland.com

Actual Reality

Ages: 11-20
Operating System: Windows or Macintosh
Actual Reality
614-433-0057
http://www.actreal.com

Developing educational software for teenagers is challenging—too childish and they won't even give it a first look, too formal and it won't get a second one. Writing software about the Bible and Christianity for teens presents an even bigger challenge. As Actual Reality proves, however, it can be done. Actual Reality is the best teen-oriented piece of software I have ever seen. The fact that it proclaims the gospel makes it nearly perfect.

The program combines interactive, cutting-edge graphics with twenty-six Christian artists who share their music, music video clips, and their personal perspectives on the Christian life. Diverse artists ranging from Caedmon's Call, the Newsboys, and T-Bone to Point of Grace, Rebecca St. James, and Jaci Velasquez, along with interviewed teens and young adults, address real issues teenagers face: sexual purity, race relations, sin, self-esteem, and the resurrection. But don't think that this is a collection of sermons. Teenagers wander through the Stuff to Know section which features a virtual city, Actual Reality Gazette, and Hidden Resources. There's also a music video section, a verse glossary, and even an animated preacher who pops up periodically with some in-your-face comments.

You'll find an example of this program's quality content and creative brilliance in the city, where a movie theater marquee boasts the title "Raised from the Dead?" Inside, Rebecca St. James comments on theories against the resurrection, including the stolen body, miraculous recovery, and mistaken grave scenarios. When you click on the stolen body, you watch a hilarious yet

Figure 18: Actual Reality

insightful animation of three disciples attempting to get past the Roman soldiers and recover Jesus' body. It vividly illustrates the foolishness of such a theory.

Actual Reality is a must for any teenager. I hope we'll see more programs like this in the future.

Logos Library System

```
Ages: 14 and up
Operating System: Windows
Logos Research Systems
800-875-6467
http://www.logos.com
```

The Logos Library System not only represents the best Bible study software on the market but also sets a new standard for electronic libraries. What makes Logos so powerful, not only for Bible study but for any reference work, is its integration of all the books into a single library with full browsing and searching features. The simple interface, book collections along the left-hand side and currently open works on the right, conceals a robust search engine by which you can search in any supported language in any single book or in all books, by keyword, phrase, topic, or complex query. Searches may be simple (finding every use of God in the New International Version translation of the Bible), more complex (tracking discussions of justification in not only the Bible but all of the reference books in your collection), or truly detailed (locating all perfect indicative occurrences of the word *teleo* in the Greek text). Clicking on individual words within the text brings up lexical definitions, morphological analysis, cross references, or further searches on that word.

The Logos Library System isn't limited to text. Graphics, maps, audio, and even video clips can be indexed and incorporated into your electronic library. The Logos Library System engine is actually free and can be downloaded from their Web site along with a few free books. You pay for the electronic book collections that populate your library. Logos and a number of other publishers

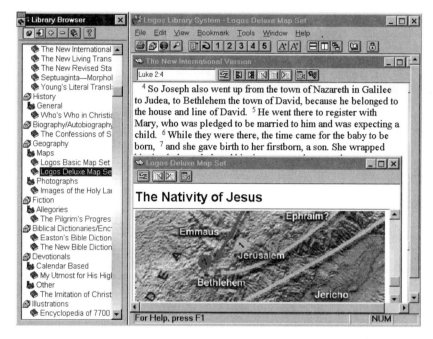

Figure 19: Logos Library System

have produced collections that seamlessly integrate numerous resources into a single digital library at a cost much more affordable than their printed counterparts. Popular collections include Logos Personal Bible Study (KJV Bible, Strong's numbers with dictionary, maps, hymns, and a devotional), Logos Scholar's Library (nine English Bibles; six commentaries; four devotionals; two dictionaries; Greek and Hebrew texts, grammars, lexicons, morphologies, and dictionaries; hymns; cross references; biographies; and maps), Anchor Bible Dictionary (the complete six-volume set, with illustrations), Cornelius Van Til Collection (all of the writings of this theologian plus more than fifty hours of his teaching and preaching), and the American Multimedia Archive (four volumes of timelines, images, maps, and audio and video clips).

There are currently over a thousand books available for the Logos Library System. Additional books and curriculum materials are currently being developed. That means soon you may be able to bring a complete educational library into your house at a fraction of the cost of printed books. Furthermore, because Logos promises free lifetime upgrades of the core searching software, you don't have to worry about your library becoming obsolete in a few years.

If you're serious about studying the Bible, or helping your older children to do so, this is the program for you. Furthermore, if you have book collections that you are interested in seeing in electronic format, I encourage you to push the publisher toward Logos. What better way to study the Word of God than with the best tools available.

Tutorial Software

Bible Foundations

```
Ages: high school and up
Operating System: Windows or Macintosh
Discovery Interactive
800-653-8333
http://www.gospelcom.net/rbc/dhp/cdrom/
```

Author Philip Yancey teaches you about the Old and New Testaments in this multimedia course study. At the heart of the program is a chronological survey of the Bible using narrative text, audio, graphics, maps, and video presentations. Exercises and questions along the way help reinforce the lessons. The presentation has the feel of a high school or college level Bible course—straightforward, detailed, and systematic. Perhaps this is why some colleges will offer credit to students who successfully complete the course and pass a comprehensive final exam. To supplement your learning, the program includes additional background material about Scripture study as well as searchable copies of the King James Version and New International Version Bibles. This solid program would work well as an introductory Bible course for older children or adults.

Encountering the New Testament

```
Ages: high school and up
Operating System: Windows or Macintosh
Baker Book House
800-877-2665
http://www.bakerbooks.com
```

This program is designed as an introductory course in the New Testament, appropriate for high school or college students, and combines a textbook and corresponding CD-ROM. The CD features a tutorial that parallels the book chapters and provides interactive review questions at the end of each section. The multimedia tutorial includes photos, maps, video clips, and a New Testament book outline. What makes this tutorial different from other programs is its inclusion of interviews with the authors of the program, who share their personal experiences with the New Testament. This program is a solid, in-depth New Testament study for beginners.

Giants of the Faith

```
Ages: 12 and up
Operating System: Windows or Macintosh
Bridgestone Multimedia Group
800-523-0988
http://www.bridgestonemultimedia.com
```

Sometimes it's difficult to get to know historical figures; students end up memorizing facts about them rather then really getting to know them. Giants of the Faith addresses that problem with the presentation of a multimedia gallery of sixteen great Christian men throughout history. The gallery is divided into four rooms: Bible translators and reformers, literary masters, evangelists and missionaries, and founders of hymnology. Each room contains a portrait of the person that, when clicked on, reveals a tutorial featuring video footage, biographical text, personal writings, and other information by and about each man of faith. This tutorial is a helpful resource if you are studying the likes of John Wycliffe, Charles Wesley, William Carey, John Bunyan, or C. S. Lewis.

Greek Tutor/Hebrew Tutor

```
Ages: high school and up
Operating System: Windows
Parsons Technology
800-779-6000
http://www.parsonstech.com
```

These tutorial programs offer straightforward presentations of Greek and Hebrew through a series of self-paced interactive lessons. Neither Greek Tutor nor Hebrew Tutor are multimedia marvels, but they are in-depth tutorials offering the equivalent of first-year college Greek and Hebrew. The programs are divided into four sections: learn, drill, exercise, and review. The learn section offers instruction in the language, with audio pronunciations of letters and words. The drill and exercise sections offer opportunities to reinforce the lesson before a quick review featuring reference charts. They make great resources for older children and adults interested in being able to read the Bible in its original languages. And you may even integrate them into the education of younger children while they are most adept at learning language.

I Love Science!

```
Ages: 7–11
Operating System: Windows or Macintosh
DK Publishing
800-986-9921
http://www.dkonline.com
```

I Love Science packages a hundred science experiments, a hundred reference screens, and a thousand questions into an entertaining and enlightening experience. Al's kitchen is the place where kids learn about chemistry, Rosie's tree house serves as the biology headquarters, and Mo's workshop is the physics lab. (Speaking of physics, and to show the wit imbedded in this program, let me reveal Mo's full name—Mo Mentum!) Each area opens with a short reading introducing children to a particular subject and then proceeds into an activity that can be a timed game or simply a leisurely exploration of key concepts. After the activity there are multiple-choice questions to answer and, to DK's credit, all answers (correct and incorrect) are explained so children understand why an answer is correct and don't merely proceed via random guessing. This program combines a variety of learning activities (reading, exploration, timed activities, games, etc.) with a breezy, witty style that really fits the targeted age group. I Love Science is worth adding to your collection. And if your child really enjoys this program, consider acquiring I Love Math and I Love Spelling as well.

Learn to Speak Series

```
Ages: 8 and up
Operating System: Windows or Macintosh
The Learning Company
800-852-2255
http://www.learningco.com
```

The Learning Company has released a fine collection of language learning software. In addition to the traditional foreign languages (French, German, Spanish), Learn to Speak versions are available for Japanese and English. A typical Learn to Speak program opens with a brief cultural introduction such as a tour of a major city and local music. The program then moves into the first of many chapters that walk you through vocabulary, reading, conversation, grammar, and pronunciation. These programs demonstrate the power of multimedia learning—integrating stories, audio narration, and video clips into lessons; including quizzes and games in practice exercises; and utilizing practical dialogues. Perhaps their most creative feature is the ability to record yourself speaking so the computer can compare your pronunciation with a native speaker. (This feature requires a microphone plugged into your computer, so programs come with a free microphone mail-in offer.)

Figure 20: Learn to Speak French

The Learn to Speak products provide a great way to independently learn another language or to reinforce your classroom studies.

Lest We Forget: A History of the Holocaust

```
Ages: high school and up
Operating System: Windows or Macintosh
Logos Research Systems
800-875-6467
http://www.logos.com
```

This program presents a powerful and disturbing reminder of the atrocities that occurred in Germany during World War II. Beginning with the rise of Hitler and the Nazis, the Holocaust, and its aftermath, this illustrated history of the Nazi oppression of the Jewish people includes narrative text, photos, maps, charts, a timeline, and audio and video clips. The presentation is largely chronological, but there are links to biographical and glossary information along the way. The opening sound of a heartbeat, audio and video footage of Hitler, photos of the ghettos and concentration camps, and haunting music make this a sobering experience. Although it's not appropriate for all ages, Lest We Forget is an excellent use of technology to affirm humanity and attempt to prevent such horrors from happening again.

Mavis Beacon Teaches Typing

```
Ages: 7 and up
Operating System: Windows or Macintosh
The Learning Company
800-852-2255
http://www.mavisbeacon.com
```

Mavis Beacon Teaches Typing simulates a traditional typing class from the rows of students seated in front of their computers down to the smiling presence and words of encouragement from the teacher, Mavis Beacon. The actual lesson screens feature the typing text and animated hands to indicate which key should be pressed next and by which finger. The customized lessons consist of text drawn from children's riddles, business letters, classic literature, or simply a collection of words and phrases that correspond to your weak areas. Mavis offers lessons and drills based on your keyboarding proficiency and habits. She also monitors whether you appear to be getting frustrated or bored, which often throws off your performance, and may suggest you play one of the seven games or call it quits for the day. She's about as close to a real instructor as you will find in a computer program.

PhonicsTutor

```
Ages: 4-9
Operating System: Windows or Macintosh
4:20 Communications
888-420-7323
http://www.phonicstutor.com
```

Based on the *Alphaphonics* book, PhonicsTutor is a straightforward reading tutorial package with little flash but lots of substance. Each lesson begins with a word list the computer reads aloud to the student, who can then request that certain words be repeated. The child then types the word while the computer pronounces each of the associated phonetic sounds. Additional activities enhance pronunciation and reading: when the computer reads a word and the student must select the proper one from a list, or when the student must pronounce a word and then listen to the computer give the proper pronunciation. More advanced lessons emphasize spelling, capitalization, and punctuation. PhonicsTutor is an excellent phonics program—it's even better than the book it's based on because the computer actually speaks to the student.

The Princeton Review: Inside the SAT and ACT Deluxe

```
Ages: high school
Operating System: Windows or Macintosh
The Learning Company
800-852-2255
http://www.learningco.com
```

The SAT (or ACT) is a rite of passage that high schoolers must endure on their way to college. It's frightening to think that so much weight is given to a single exam, but Inside the SAT and ACT will help ease your fear in two ways. First, it offers ten full-length practice tests plus hundreds of individual drills to improve specific skills. By identifying strong areas and sharpening weak ones, and by giving students the opportunity to become familiar with the test itself, Inside the SAT and ACT lowers anxiety and raises scores. However, the program goes beyond drill and practice by including test-taking strategies, insight into how the test is written, and a study calendar to plan for the big day. The program also features college selection counseling, financial aid information, and an admissions deadline reminder. Inside the SAT and ACT is a wise purchase for any pre-college student.

Reader Rabbit's Complete Learn to Read System

```
Ages: 3-7
Operating System: Windows or Macintosh
The Learning Company
800-852-2255
http://www.learningco.com
```

The Learning Company has produced a winner with Reader Rabbit's Complete Learn to Read System. Unlike most reading computer programs, the Complete Learn to Read System couples a quality software package with a multitude of additional teaching tools. In addition to the two CD-ROMs, the Complete Learn to Read System includes two sets of flashcards (alphabet and words), an alphabet poster, seven storybooks containing a total of twenty-six stories, a student workbook, and a parents' guide. The program then integrates all of the various tools into a four-step learning process—letters, sounds, rods, and sentences—which can be approached through either a directed quest to restore letters and words to Wordville or less systematic games and activities. The program combines phonics and limited word recognition approaches toward the goal of reading and comprehending sentences. Progress reports are available for parents, including a running record of areas that children are struggling with, and printable certificates not only recognize achievement but actually list the words that students have mastered. Overall, the Complete Learn to Read System clearly demonstrates the power of combining computerized and traditional learning approaches to help kids learn. And it's a whole lot of fun too!

Reality: The Prelude to an Answer

```
Ages: high school and up
Operating System: Windows
Nexus Studios
888-336-3987
http://www.nexusstudios.com
```

This program is essentially a multimedia CD-ROM version of the video series by the same name which is hosted by Dr. Michael Green. As such, it is primarily a series of high-tech lectures about various questions including who is God, who is Jesus, and is there really any meaning to life. As video clips roll of Dr. Green discussing these questions, a transcript of his words scrolls alongside selected words linked to articles with more information about a given topic. The program also features search capabilities, personal note storage, and quizzes. What makes this program noteworthy isn't the multimedia features as much as the depth of information presented. This isn't shallow Bible study—it offers in-depth insight into practical theology and philosophy.

Robinson Self-Teaching Curriculum

```
Ages: 4–18
Operating System: Windows or Macintosh
Oregon Institute of Science and Medicine
248-740-2697
http://www.robinsoncurriculum.com
```

This is an unusual entry in that while it is a self-teaching curriculum, much of it is designed to be printed out and used in hardcopy form. After the death of his wife, Dr. Art Robinson raised six children who taught themselves based on a comprehensive curriculum his wife had developed before her untimely death. This is that curriculum. The package is a complete K–12 curriculum, sans math (users are instructed to purchase Saxon Math separately), published on twenty-two CD-ROMs. Included on the CDs are the following: more than 250 illustrated books covering literature, science, economics, general education, and pleasure reading; the 1911 *Encyclopedia Britannica;* the 1913 *Webster's Dictionary;* examinations; vocabulary words; flashcards; current science texts; and a hundred pages of instruction to parents. The books can be viewed online or, as is generally preferred, printed. Therefore, despite the inclusion of a few interactive quizzes, the CDs are primarily a high-tech way of storing hundreds of thousands of pages of text. Although both the curriculum content and teaching philosophy may be at times lacking, this program is noteworthy because it bundles a complete K–12 Christian curriculum into a single package that includes extensive counsel to parents. Therefore, the Robinson curriculum is worth considering for adoption or simply as a reference collection to add to your library.

Switched-On Schoolhouse

```
Ages: 10-17
Operating System: Windows
Alpha Omega Publications
800-622-3070
http://www.switched-onschoolhouse.com
```

Switched-On Schoolhouse (SOS) is a multimedia version of Alpha Omega's homeschooling curriculum. Like its printed counterpart, SOS covers the Bible, science, language arts, math, history, and geography. Each CD-ROM is a complete self-contained curriculum featuring all of the lessons, activities, exams, and reference materials associated with that unit. Typical units contain narrative text, vocabulary, contemporary applications, graphics, and audio and video clips. After each lesson there is a series of true or false, fill-in-the-blank, scrambled word, matching, or short answer questions for the student to answer. If the focus learning feature is activated, the student cannot continue to the next section until he or she has mastered the current one. SOS provides focused tutoring and review prior to repeating missed questions, and only after the student achieves proficiency can he or she move on. Unlike many computerized curricula, the SOS evaluation portion isn't limited to true or false or multiple choice questions but includes matching, crossword puzzles, fill-in-the-blanks, and even essay questions. In teacher mode, parents can choose between letter and percentage grades, enable the focus learning feature, determine the penalty for misspelled words, weigh the relative value of different exercises, view lessons and exams with the appropriate answer key, and track student performance in an electronic gradebook. With grades five through eleven currently avail-

MATHEMATICS 701: SETS AND NUMBERS
SETS: INTRODUCTION

In this unit you will learn about sets and how to perform such basic operations as intersection and union of sets. Visualizing sets with Venn diagrams will be informative and fun.

Numbers are shown in many forms: early number systems, our decimal number system, and various other number bases. Egyptian numerals, Greek numerals, Roman numerals, and Arabic numerals represent early number systems. The ideas of place value and powers of ten will be covered in decimal numerals.

When collections of objects or numbers are organized or have something in common, they are called *sets*. Concepts of sets and operations with sets will be studied in this section.

CONCEPTS

In the study of sets, basic terms, types of sets, and uses of sets will give you a better understanding of what sets are and how to work with them.

A set is a collection or group of objects. Sets can involve almost anything.

Figure 21: Switched-On Schoolhouse

able, Switched-On Schoolhouse is a solid step toward the development of a comprehensive K–12 Christian curriculum.

Discovery Software

A.D.A.M. The Inside Story

```
Ages: 10-14
Operating System: Windows or Macintosh
A.D.A.M. Software
800-755-2326
http://www.adam.com
```

Using 3-D anatomical images, you can explore virtually every aspect of the human body. The Inside Story is divided into five major sections: basic anatomy, family scrapbook, the Quizmeister, animation, and Internet access. Basic anatomy, probably the most fascinating section, enables you to examine the human body by selecting and peeling away layer after layer. You can zoom in, change viewing angles, and continue to delve further into the multiple layers that make up the body. There are also additional 3-D explorations of the heart, brain, and lungs as well as links to the family scrapbook. The family scrapbook offers a multimedia introduction to the twelve major human body systems with the option to visit the Quizmeister, an interactive question section written in teenage vernacular. The animation section offers video segments with more information about the human body. The program also includes a connection to the corresponding Web site that offers even more information. Such a connection, I believe, will become an increasingly more common feature in future educational software. Finally, The Inside Story includes a modesty option that enables parents to put fig leaves over appropriate anatomical features.

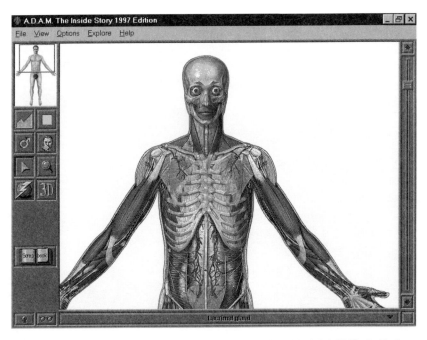

Figure 22: A.D.A.M. The Inside Story

The Dead Sea Scrolls Revealed

```
Ages: high school and up
Operating System: Windows or Macintosh
Logos Research Systems
800-875-6467
http://www.logos.com
```

For students of the Bible, the Dead Sea Scrolls have always been an interesting combination of scholarly study and mystery. Why were the scrolls hidden in a cave by the Dead Sea? What was the Qumran community like and what role did they have in the writing and preservation of the scrolls? What did the scrolls say and how does the text relate to the Bible? Logos's Dead Sea Scrolls Revealed offers a multimedia journey of discovery in search of answers to such questions. The program's opening screen presents six areas of exploration: history, location, the discovery, scroll work, the debates, and the scrolls themselves. From there you become an archaeologist, exploring and uncovering secrets found within by clicking on various objects. You are rewarded with narrative text, geographical graphics, digitized photos of the scrolls with translation, video clips of scholarly commentary, and even an animated fly-through of the Qumran buildings. Although the content and design limits this learning experience to older children and adults, it's a fascinating journey.

Life's Greatest Mysteries

```
Ages: 10-18
Operating System: Windows or Macintosh
A.D.A.M. Software
800-755-2326
http://www.adam.com
```

This is a rather unusual program but one that many children enjoy. British host Bob Winkle leads children through a quest to answer questions about the body, curiosity, the mind, and sickness. The animated host harnesses text, audio, photography, and video to answer such questions as: what causes goose bumps, how do we remember things, and why are some people left-handed while most are right-handed. Along the way children can play memory games, view optical illusions, or read some definitions from the dictionary. This program fits well with children's natural curiosity and might even answer some of those questions that have been stumping you.

The New Way Things Work

```
Ages: 7 and up
Operating System: Windows or Macintosh
DK Publishing
800-986-9921
http://www.dkonline.com
```

David Macaulay's classic book makes for a fascinating journey into the way things work. David and his woolly mammoth friend serve as commentators, and comic relief, for your explorations into the details of machines, inventors, history, science, and the digital domain. From toasters and turbines to cell phones and GPS satellites, The New Way Things Work lets children learn about the inner workings of numerous everyday objects. Although the program doesn't expand on the book as much as I would like, it remains an enjoyable learning experience for kids and adults alike.

Nine Month Miracle

```
Ages: 3-18
Operating System: Windows or Macintosh
A.D.A.M. Software
800-755-2326
http://www.adam.com
```

In Nine Month Miracle you meet a modern Adam and Eve who, along with a group of medical experts, guide you on a nine-month tour of Eve's pregnancy. Beginning with conception, you follow the development of the baby using real-life video, animations, and some amazing in-utero photography in the interactive family album. Children and adults watch the baby grow, learn about when each of the major organs develop, see how the baby gets food, view an ultrasound, and even watch a baby being born. Similar to The Inside Story, Nine Month Miracle features a modesty setting that locks out conception and delivery material and covers male and female genitals with fig leaves. While most of Nine Month Miracle is geared toward older children, the program includes a section called "A Child's View of Pregnancy" that is geared for the younger crowd. You should preview this program prior to letting your child use it, or perhaps work through the interactive family album together. But this is an excellent presentation of the wonder of new life. Although it's done from a secular point of view, you cannot help but worship God as you see a baby develop so precisely.

A Walk in the Footsteps of Jesus

```
Ages: 10 and up
Operating System: Windows or Macintosh
Parsons Technology
800-779-6000
http://www.parsonstech.com
```

Jerusalem comes alive through a unique technology called PhotoBubbles. PhotoBubbles are 360-degree pictures that enable you to view the Holy Land as if you were really there. You can look up, down, left, right, or even catch a peripheral glance. As you wander through the major locations from Jesus' life—including Nazareth, the Jordan River, the Mount of Transfiguration, the garden tomb, and many more—you can zoom in for close-up looks or back up to view the scene at a distance. As you explore you can read, listen, or watch video clips of information related to the site you are viewing. The clips include corresponding Bible verses, stories, and maps. A Walk in the Footsteps of Jesus is a great way to see Israel without leaving home.

Figure 23: A Walk in the Footsteps of Jesus

Edutainment Software

Amazing Expedition Bible CD-ROM

```
Ages: 8–12
Operating System: Windows or Macintosh
Baker Book House
800-877-2665
http://www.bakerbooks.com
```

This program is the counterpart to the printed *Amazing Expedition Bible*. The program contains sixty-two Bible stories with a mixture of text and graphics you can choose to read or have the computer read to you. A timeline linking all of the stories together makes this program particularly powerful. As you read each story the timeline at the top of the screen shows where the story fits within biblical and historical chronology. Furthermore, there is also a series of categories such as people and daily life, music, visual arts, and science, technology, and growth that can be selected for further information. For instance, if you select science, technology, and growth while reading about Shadrach, Meshach, and Abednego you learn about Nebuchadnezzar's famous hanging gardens. The interconnection of the biblical stories with the surrounding world is a great feature of this program. The program also contains mysteries, movies, fun facts, and an exploration game to keep children in the Bible.

babyWOW!

```
Ages: 9 months to 3 years
Operating System: Windows or Macintosh
BowWow House
888-899-0798
http://www.babywow.com
```

For those who are interested in lapware, babyWOW is perhaps the best program available. The program covers a variety of concepts including colors, words, shapes, and music, all at an infant level. For instance, the Vocabulary section displays a single photograph on the screen and audibly identifies the picture to the child. Similarly, the Basic Colors activity paints the screen a solid shade while the computer speaks the corresponding color. The Photo Albums section contains numerous high-quality color photographs for your infant to view. For these and all the other sections, such as Peekaboo and What Is It, simply banging on the keyboard advances you to the next entry. babyWOW will speak in eight different languages including English, French, Spanish, and Japanese. The highlights of the program are its simplicity, which is appropriate for the age group, and the collection of beautiful high-quality photographs.

The Beginners Bible Series

```
Ages: 3–8
Operating System: Windows or Macintosh
Baker Book House
800-877-2665
http://www.bakerbooks.com
```

If you're one of the millions of families with a copy of *The Beginners Bible,* you might want to consider the corresponding computer software: Noah's Ark Activity Center, The Birth of Jesus Activity Center, and The Story of Easter. The Noah's Ark and Birth of Jesus programs feature a variety of educational activities. While your children help Noah prepare for the flood or an angel prepare for baby Jesus, they learn the Bible through jigsaw puzzles, sing-along songs, trivia questions, mazes, matching games, melody makers, and even coloring pages. The Story of Easter uses an interactive book approach including animated pages, video clips, sing-along songs, and fun Easter facts. The Easter software is a bit less flexible than the others because you cannot save your progress and return to the program at a later time. However, since all three programs use the same artwork and text as *The Beginners Bible,* they make a fun and educational complement to your child's devotions.

Blaster Learning Series

```
Ages: 4–12
Operating System: Windows or Macintosh
Knowledge Adventure
800-542-4240
http://www.knowledgeadventure.com
```

Math Blaster, Reading Blaster, and Writing Blaster can be purchased individually or bundled into the Blaster Learning System 3R's package. The Math Blaster programs all feature a space motif where you are challenged with increasingly difficult arcade-style games in which you must use your math prowess to save the day.

From basic numbers to pre-algebra, Math Blaster programs provide a fun alternative to repetitive math drills. The Reading Blaster series combines interactive stories, game shows, role-play adventures, and other challenges to reinforce reading. The programs range from introductory reading with phonics to vocabulary, comprehension, and grammar. Writing Blaster is a recent addition to the collection and combines letter, word, and vocabulary drills with design tools and templates that enable your child to create greeting cards, poems, and stories. All the programs contain multiple levels of difficulty which can be adjusted to suit your child.

Carmen Sandiego Series

```
Ages: 8-14
Operating System: Windows or Macintosh
Broderbund Software
800-548-1798
http://www.broderbund.com
```

Carmen Sandiego, "the first lady of thievery," journeys around the country, the world, and even through time, stealing treasures along the way. Your mission is to track her down, capture any of her criminal associates, recover anything that she's hidden, and ultimately nab Carmen herself. For example, in Where in Time Is Carmen Sandiego you must travel through time and solve eighteen different cases by speaking with various historical characters to uncover the stolen item and find the thief's hiding place. Once you've solved each of the cases, which occur in a variety of different time periods, you must catch Carmen through a final chase that draws from information learned in the previous eighteen. Other programs in the series include Carmen Sandiego Math Detective, Carmen Sandiego Word Detective, and the original Where in the World Is Carmen Sandiego. The Carmen Sandiego series combines teaching (such as geography, history, math) and problem-solving challenges all set within a compelling storyline. The programs are educational and enjoyable—an ideal combination.

ClueFinders' 3rd Grade Adventures

```
Ages: 7-9
Operating System: Windows or Macintosh
The Learning Company
800-852-2255
http://www.learningco.com
```

ClueFinders' 3rd Grade Adventure offers an Indiana Jones–style adventure through a mysterious rain forest. Horace Pythagorus, the uncle of one of the kid explorers, has disappeared along with numerous animals. Rumor has it that a ravenous monster—Mathra—might be responsible. To rescue Dr. Pythagorus the two explorers must find the keys to the Lost City. Along the way you must navigate the Monkey Kingdom and conquer a series of math problems, crack the logic puzzles in the Goo Lagoon, practice geography in the Jungle Canopy, and use science and language arts skills to triumph in the Lost City. By wrapping the activities within a mystery and setting the adventure within a cartoon-style jungle, ClueFinders provides an excellent balance between engaging fun and challenging learning. It's a worthwhile supplement to your third-grade curriculum.

DroidWorks

```
Ages: 10 and up
Operating System: Windows or Macintosh
Lucas Learning
888-887-7909
http://www.droidworks.com
```

From the Star Wars universe comes an excellent combination of scientific strategy and entertainment. Your mission is to create a friendly droid that can infiltrate an evil Empire droid factory and reprogram their droids. Your challenge begins in the droid workshop where you have eighty-seven different parts that can be combined to create millions of different droids. The 3-D holographic workshop lets you view the specifications for each of the parts, assemble them into a droid, and examine your result from

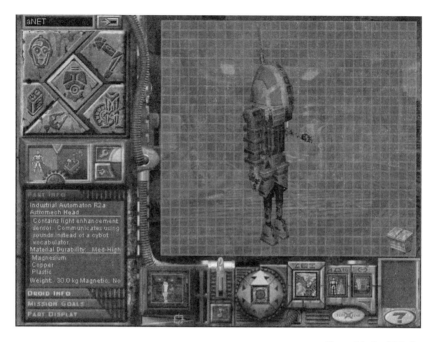

Figure 24: DroidWorks

any angle. This aspect of the program is both fun and fascinating even on its own. Once you build your droid you set out on the various legs of your mission, where your droid faces various physical challenges while you are confronted with different mental puzzles. I had a lot of fun with DroidWorks and am convinced that it's a great program for the engineer in any child.

Explore the Bible: The Life of Christ

```
Ages: 7 and up
Operating System: Windows or Macintosh
Discovery Interactive
800-653-8333
http://www.gospelcom.net/rbc/dhp/cdrom/
```

This multimedia adventure challenges the student to explore the life of Jesus Christ with a series of forty lessons from his birth

Figure 25: Explore the Bible: The Life of Christ

through his resurrection. As students explore Professor Newheart's Office and the Castle of Hidden Clues to find the keys to two mysterious chests, they must successfully complete lessons about significant events in Jesus' life, his incarnation, biblical history, the geography of Israel, and the books of the New Testament. Through reading, pictures, and video segments, they learn about Jesus and are challenged with questions to demonstrate their mastery. Successfully answering the corresponding lesson questions results in a mastery certificate and a piece of information needed to unlock the two chests. This program presents quality educational lessons within an enticing multimedia environment.

Jump Start Series

```
Ages: 1-12
Operating System: Windows or Macintosh
```

Knowledge Adventure
800-542-4240
http://www.jumpstart.com

The Jump Start series, which goes from Jump Start Baby through Jump Start 6th Grade, is one of the best edutainment series available. Jump Start Grade School, which bundles kindergarten through fifth grade, is a good purchase for families with multiple children. Each grade level offers a challenging storyline that incorporates numerous learning activities. For instance, in Jump Start 3rd Grade a smart and devious girl has altered reality to conform to her unusual desires (e.g., because cake and ice cream make her happy, nurses give cake and ice cream to cure sick people). Your challenge is to capture her reality-altering robots, which are loose on an island laboratory, by successfully mastering challenges in history, science, grammar, math, art, and logic. The computer automatically adjusts the difficulty based on your child's performance, and you can track your child's progress through each level. My only concern with this otherwise excellent series is that some of the themes are questionable. For example, Jump Start 4th Grade takes place on a haunted island with ghosts and mummies. However, it would be unfortunate to condemn the whole series for a few disconcerting themes. Overall this series represents a creative learning tool for students.

KidSpeak 10-in-1 Language Learning

Ages: 6 and up
Operating System: Windows or Macintosh
Transparent Language
603-465-2230
http://www.transparent.com

KidSpeak takes a different approach to language learning than most computer programs or traditional classes do. Using a series of games, puzzles, and songs, KidSpeak immerses your child in a different language. In fact, KidSpeak 10-in-1 Lan-

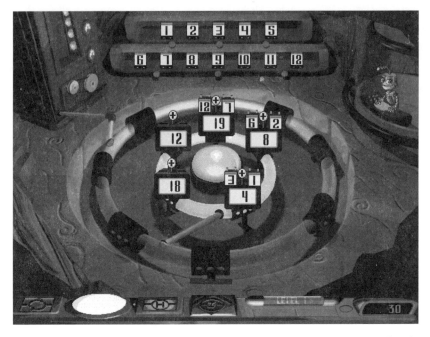

Figure 26: Jump Start 3rd Grade

guage Learning offers your child the opportunity to be immersed in any one of ten different languages—Spanish, French, Italian, German, Japanese, Indonesian, Korean, Hebrew, Portuguese, or Chinese. There are no drills, no translations, and no formal exercises; rather your child is paired up with a cartoon character who speaks only the designated language. Each language has five different activity modules that cover the alphabet, numbers, animals, backpack (which covers common vocabulary such as food, clothing, and transportation), and a birthday party. KidSpeak also includes practice worksheets you can print out and use away from the computer. This engaging program offers an innovative way of learning a second (or third or fourth) language that matches the way we learned our first language. It's definitely worth considering if you want to start language learning early.

Figure 27: Let's Go Read!

Let's Go Read! An Island Adventure *and* Let's Go Read! 2 An Ocean Adventure

    Ages: 4–7
    Operating System: Windows or Macintosh
    Edmark
    800-691-2986
    http://www.edmark.com

As with similar reading programs, there are plenty of instructional activities, phonics, games, and interactive books in the Let's Go Read programs. However, the Let's Go Read products take reading software to a new level by incorporating speech recognition technology into these two edutainment packages. An Island Adventure comes with a microphone and baseball cap your child can wear on her head. Thanks to the microphone and speech recognition, the software incorporates voice-activated activities such as asking the child to pronounce letters, words, or phrases. The computer responds based on the accuracy of your child's speech and can even play back his or her responses. These two products are perhaps the most innovative reading programs on the market today and are well worth the investment, as either a teaching tool or simply fun reinforcement.

Madeline Thinking Games Deluxe

```
Ages: 5 and up
Operating System: Windows or Macintosh
The Learning Company
800-852-2255
http://www.learningco.com
```

Recently a number of publishers have attempted to produce software that appeals specifically to girls. This program featuring the popular character Madeline does just that. Madeline Thinking Games Deluxe is a collection of over fifty fun activities that help girls reinforce learning and build their problem-solving skills. As Madeline guides you through her French schoolhouse, and then throughout Europe, you encounter a series of puzzles. Activities include matching French and Spanish vocabulary skills, navigating a maze in the garden where her dog, Genevieve, has gotten lost, finding the music box that plays "Pop Goes the Weasel," and arranging a set of pictures in proper chronological sequence. The program also includes an interior design section where users wallpaper, carpet, and furnish an empty room, as well as songs, videos, printable postcards, and award certificates. This delightful program offers three difficulty levels.

Myst/Riven

```
Ages: 11 and up
Operating System: Windows or Macintosh
Broderbund Software
800-548-1798
http://www.broderbund.com
```

Figure 28: New Kids Point & Play Bible

Myst is the all-time best-selling CD-ROM computer game; Riven is its sequel. These nonviolent adventure games combine breathtakingly realistic 3-D imagery with challenging mysteries. Both programs feature animations, video clips, and a complete musical score. Myst starts simply—you find a book entitled *Myst*—and the next thing you know, you're transported into an alternate world where your first challenge is to figure out what you're doing there. Riven is equally intriguing and even more challenging than its predecessor. Children and adults can spend hours engaging their problem-solving skills by wandering through the worlds of Myst and Riven.

New Kids Point & Play Bible on CD-ROM

```
Ages: 4–8
Operating System: Windows or Macintosh
Baker Book House
```

800-877-2665
http://www.bakerbooks.com

The New Kids Point & Play Bible CD-ROM contains sixty interactive Bible stories for your child to enjoy. Your child can read each illustrated story, or listen as the computer reads, while searching for the hidden animations that pop up when clicked on. Each story has a corresponding puzzle, matching game, coloring page, or other activity. Children can also click on the Big Idea button to view the main point and practical application of the Bible story. This is a fun way for little children to learn about the Bible and enjoy spending time in the Word.

Pinball Science

Ages: 8–14
Operating System: Windows
DK Publishing
800-986-9921
http://www.dkonline.com

From David Macaulay, the author of *The New Way Things Work,* comes a similarly fascinating (and even more fun) program that combines learning about science with constructing your own pinball machines. The inventor of mammoth-sized pinball machines and his assistant, Mammoth, have disappeared, and you must restore three pinball machines to working order to rescue the wayward pair. By reading through the inventor's journal, answering science questions, and successfully placing giant pinball components, such as faucets, magnets, and springs, in place you help rescue the amusing duo and get to play some mean games of pinball in the process. This highly creative program is quite fun and serves as a nice introduction to science and problem solving.

Reader Rabbit's Preschool/Reader Rabbit's Kindergarten

Ages: 2–6
Operating System: Windows or Macintosh

Figure 29: Reader Rabbit's Kindergarten

The Learning Company
800-852-2255
http://www.learningco.com

Virtually every program geared to this young age group must have a significant entertainment component, so these Reader Rabbit programs combine fun and learning. Specifically, the preschool program emphasizes number recognition, counting, shapes, letter and sound recognition, pattern matching, and memory skills. Reader Rabbit's Kindergarten focuses on counting, seasons, sorting, basic math, following directions, and sharing. The programs feature kid-friendly graphics, music, and songs to round out the learning experience. Kids will enjoy working through the challenges—especially since there is a final reward at the end of each program—and will learn throughout the process.

SimCity Series

```
Ages: all
Operating System: Windows or Macintosh
Maxis
800-245-4525
http://www.maxis.com
```

The SimCity series has been leading the way in educational software for many years and is still one of the best around. From the original SimCity Classic and its sequels, SimCity 2000 and 3000, to the more specialized programs such as SimCoptor, Sim-Safari, and SimTown, these simulation games are both fun and educational. SimCity Classic, for example, gives you a plot of land to develop. As mayor you oversee housing construction, build industry and commercial sites, construct power plants, lay highways and railroads, place police and fire stations around town, and manage the development of the overall community. As time progresses you must deal with budgets, taxes, crime, pollution, traffic, population changes, natural disasters, public works maintenance, and even public opinion. You don't really win or lose SimCity (unless you get ousted as mayor). Rather it's a fascinating exercise in urban development that unfolds according to your decisions. Other programs in the series follow a similar real-life approach to issues such as flying a helicoptor or exploring the jungle. The programs are easy enough that they're often used in school classrooms while being sophisticated enough that adults develop and exchange simulations over the Internet. Be aware that these programs aren't without their ethical dilemmas: In the urban development programs you possess godlike power as mayor and success is measured strictly in economic and quantitative terms. SimLife and SimEarth are particularly problematic because they are built on an evolutionary perspective. However, parents may rise to the challenge and use the SimCity series as an opportunity to help develop in their children a biblical worldview.

Figure 30: SimCity 3000

Trail Adventure Collection

Ages: 10 and up
Operating System: Windows or Macintosh
The Learning Company
800-852-2255
http://www.learningco.com

The Trail Adventure Collection combines five individual programs: The Yukon Trail, Explore Yellowstone, The Amazon Trail, Mayaquest—The Mystery Trail, and Africa Trail. Each program involves a journey you must complete. You may find yourself striking it rich during the 1897 Gold Rush or participating in a twelve-thousand-mile bike trek through Africa. As you journey you learn about history, natural sciences, geography, and culture as you conquer the many obstacles you encounter along the way. The graphic quality varies widely (The Yukon Trail has 2-D cartoons, Mayaquest incorporates 3-D graphics, and Africa Trail features photos and video clips), but the educational experiences are all excellent.

Authoring Software

The American Girls Premiere

```
Ages: 8–12
Operating System: Windows or Macintosh
The Learning Company
800-852-2255
http://www.learningco.com
```

Is your daughter a fan of the American Girls—Felicity, Josefina, Kirsten, Addy, Samantha, and Molly? If so, she'll love The American Girls Premiere. This excellent program allows you to create a live-action American Girls play. After doing some preliminary research you select a character to star in the play, choose her scenic backdrop, and begin to create the production. Then add additional characters, costumes, and props to round out the overall scene. Once the stage is set you can write a script and record dialog by either using your own voice via a microphone or letting the computer read the lines. As you bring the story together you assume the director's role and instruct the characters what actions to perform and which emotions to use. Finally, round out the production with appropriate music and lighting, print your playbill, and enjoy the show. Tutorials, sample plays, and play starters help you get warmed up. The American Girls Premiere is a superb program worth exploring.

ClickArt Christian Publishing Suite

```
Ages: 7 and up
Operating System: Windows
Broderbund Software
```

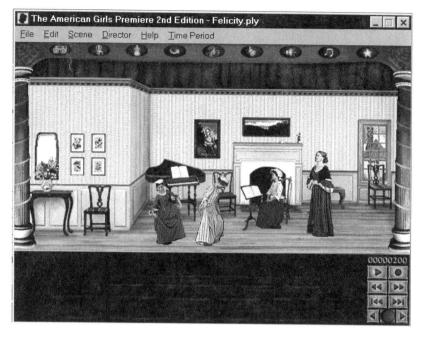

Figure 31: The American Girls Premiere

800-548-1798
http://www.broderbund.com

This publishing suite contains over ten thousand Christian graphics (in categories such as Bible stories, symbols, prayers, Scriptures, holidays) as well as photos, artistic alphabets, and True-Type fonts. While the graphics by themselves are a nice resource for children, the ClickArt Christian Publishing Suite also includes Print Shop Press Writer and Announcements for design work. Print Shop Press Writer lets you create posters, bulletins, flyers, newsletters, and other publications from more than a hundred easy-to-use templates. Announcements add the ability to create certificates, calendars, cards, envelopes, and more. Your family can use the ClickArt Christian Publishing Suite for everything from school assignments to Christmas cards. Although Kid Pix Studio Deluxe is easier for younger children, this is a nice com-

Figure 32: Kid Pix Studio Deluxe

bination of high-quality authoring tools with appropriate Christian-themed graphics.

Kid Pix Studio Deluxe

```
Ages: 3-12
Operating System: Windows or Macintosh
Broderbund Software
800-548-1798
http://www.broderbund.com
```

An artist's dream, Kid Pix Studio Deluxe combines six different creativity programs: a drawing and painting program, an animation studio, a theater stage, computer marionettes, a movie viewer, and a slideshow designer. The program also includes thousands of stamps, hundreds of clip art pictures, maps, sounds, and patterns. Children (and young-at-heart adults) can create cartoon strips, fun pictures, stylish photos, movies, greeting cards, puppet shows, and much more. This is a must-have program for anyone interested in creating artwork on the computer.

LESSONmaker Youthworker's Library

```
Ages: high school and up
Operating System: Windows or Macintosh
NavPress Software
800-888-9898
http://www.navpress.com
```

This program combines three major resources—WORDsearch Bible study software, the Youthworker Encyclopedia, and LESSONmaker Bible study developer—into a single useful tool with more than 150 youth meeting kits. Each kit contains exercises grouped as starters, discussions, challenges, and extras, as well as related materials including Bible verses, book introductions, and outlines. These resources, along with Bible passages, maps, and study questions, can be pulled together into a custom Bible study to be printed for you and your students. The Youthworker Encyclopedia is a database containing over a thousand pages of facts, opinions, case studies, and discussion ideas covering 295 youth-oriented topics. The youth focus of this package makes the LESSONmaker component particularly beneficial to parents desiring to make the Bible practical in the day-to-day lives of their children.

Microsoft FrontPage

```
Ages: 10 and up
Operating System: Windows
Microsoft
425-882-8080
http://www.microsoft.com
```

Although you can easily create basic World Wide Web pages using most word processing programs, such as Microsoft Word or

Works, FrontPage is a dedicated Web authoring tool. There are templates and wizards (step-by-step guides) to assist beginners with the creation of their first Web pages and more sophisticated tools to please the advanced Web developer. If you're interested in creating a family site online, or your children want to build their own Web pages, FrontPage is an excellent choice.

Microsoft Works Suite

```
Ages: 10 and up
Operating System: Windows
Microsoft
425-882-8080
http://www.microsoft.com
```

No authoring collection is complete without a word processor package, and Works fills that need plus much more. Microsoft Works Suite is a collection of programs including word processor, spreadsheet, database, drawing, and communication applications all integrated with a single interface. (These programs are essentially scaled down versions of Microsoft's Office applications.) The suite features a number of templates, help assistants, and wizards to help you accomplish common tasks. However, the Works suite also contains a full copy of Microsoft Word as well as Microsoft Money, Studio Graphics, and the Encarta encyclopedia. Since Word is the most popular word processor, you can begin with the Works word processor and then step up to Word at any time. Furthermore, the combination of Word and Studio Graphics is noteworthy because they provide all of the necessary tools for designing your own World Wide Web pages.

Reference Software

Baker Bible Encyclopedia for Kids on CD-ROM

```
Ages: 8–12
Operating System: Windows or Macintosh
```

```
Baker Book House
800-877-2665
http://www.bakerbooks.com
```

This children's reference collection actually contains the text of the *Baker Bible Encyclopedia, Bible Dictionary, Bible Handbook, Book of Bible People*, and *Book of Bible Travel.* This program offers an alphabetical list of topics, grouped by category (words, people, places, etc.), that children can browse or search through. When an entry is selected, the narrative text is presented along with cartoon graphics, video clips, sound effects, and hypertext links to other entries. The program includes phonetic spelling and audio pronunciation of each entry and a customizable age-appropriate interface. This is a good child-centered reference collection to help your kids better understand the Bible.

Christian History Interactive

```
Ages: 11 and up
Operating System: Windows
Christianity Today Incorporated
800-806-7798
http://www.christianity.net
```

This program can work as a stand-alone or as an add-on to the Logos Library System. It contains the complete contents of fifty issues of *Christian History* magazine. Every article, timeline, piece of artwork, photograph, and map can be browsed or searched by keyword. The printed magazine has always been a fine educational resource, and this electronic library makes it affordable and convenient to purchase a complete collection of *Christian History.*

Family Tree Maker Deluxe Edition

```
Ages: 10 and up
Operating System: Windows
Broderbund Software
```

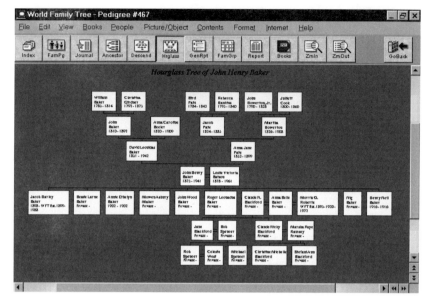

Figure 33: Family Tree Maker Deluxe

800-548-1798
http://www.broderbund.com

Family Tree Maker Deluxe combines an authoring package with a vast array of genealogical reference material. Using standard forms, you enter names, dates and locations of births, marriages, and deaths, and other facts about each person in your family. Other forms provide additional information such as employment history, baptism, or place of burial, and there are additional windows for free-form information. Photos, graphics, video clips, or other artwork can be included in your family tree. As you enter each person relative to others already entered, the program monitors your effort to catch obvious mistakes (such as a birth year later than a marriage date) and automatically grows your family tree. Once populated your family tree can be browsed, searched, or printed in a number of formats. Family Tree Maker Deluxe also includes nine CDs of genealogical reference material including a FamilyFinder index of 170 million people (and their corresponding records), a Social Security death index with 55 million records, over a million marriage records, and 27,000 actual family trees linking 15 million people together. The program also has an Internet component where you can publish your family tree or find additional information about genealogy. Therefore, in addition to helping you record your family's history, you might uncover even more branches thanks to the wealth of information in Family Tree Maker Deluxe. If you have any interest in your family history, this is the program to use.

Grolier Multimedia Encyclopedia

```
Ages: 10 and up
Operating System: Windows or Macintosh
Grolier Interactive
203-797-3530
http://www.grolier.com
```

Most popular CD-ROM encyclopedias are quality products. Grolier stands out, though, with its solid balance of substantive content, multimedia components (including 360-degree photos, videos, animations, guided tours, maps, and timelines), and ease of use for younger children. The encyclopedia also has an Internet feature that lets you view new and updated articles, relevant Web sites, and the complete contents of *Encyclopedia Americana* and *The New Book of Knowledge*.

Logos Bible Atlas

```
Ages: all
Operating System: Windows
Logos Research Systems
800-875-6467
http://www.logos.com
```

Far more than a computerized collection of 2-D maps, Logos Bible Atlas features an interactive map where you can click on a name or location and instantly get a pop-up window showing corresponding scriptural and archaeological information. You can view the same map at different periods in history to see how the city names and countries developed. You can view a fully-rotatable 3-D topological map of Palestine, view elevation, zoom in or out, or measure the distance between any two points. There's even a topical map feature that includes multiple subject maps of various episodes within biblical history (e.g., the military conquests of Joshua or journeys of Paul). Maps may be printed or exported into paint or drawing programs. Logos Bible Atlas is a quality stand-alone resource or can be integrated into the Logos Library System.

QuickVerse Multimedia Life Application Bible

```
Ages: 10 and up
Operating System: Windows
Tyndale New Media
630-668-8310
http://www.tyndale.com
```

This program takes a different twist on Bible software. Rather than emphasizing a reference library, like the Logos Library System, the QuickVerse Multimedia Life Application Bible is meant to be more devotional in nature. The program features the New Living Translation and over ten thousand life application notes that help the reader apply Scripture to daily living. Furthermore, there are topical articles and personality profiles to round out one's understanding of the Bible and one-year Bible reading plans to help people stay disciplined. But this program goes beyond mere text and includes thirty PhotoBubble images (using the same technology found in A Walk in the Footsteps of Jesus) plus pictures, maps, and artwork. For those who prefer listening, there are more than 150 dramatic readings, and every word in the Bible can be pronounced for you with a simple click. These features make this electronic Bible a preferred devotional choice for both children and adults.

For More Information

I hope you are excited about using the computer in your child's education. Despite recent advances in educational technology and the rapid growth and development of the Internet, we're still in the early stages of educational computing. Resources will continue to develop, and in the coming years we will see an increase in the number and depth of educational software products available. Furthermore, the next generation Internet (often called Internet2) will become an integral component of most educational programs. Distance learning will also continue to grow and be used often, both as a substitute for and a supplement to more traditional educational programs. The future growth of educational computing is exciting to contemplate because, if it's handled well, our children will be its benefactors.

If you're interested in finding more information about educational computing, I encourage you to examine some of the magazines that address this topic:

- *Christian Computing* (800-456-1868, http://www.ccmag.com)—This monthly magazine features how-to articles, software reviews, Web resources, and other information about computing from a Christian perspective.

- *Christianity Online* (888-432-5828, `http://www.christi anity.net`)—From Christianity Today, Inc. comes this bimonthly magazine covering software, multimedia, and the Internet from a Christian perspective. Features an educational computing column.
- *FamilyPC* (303-665-8930, `http://www.familypc.com`)— Although not a Christian magazine, this excellent monthly resource provides information about family computer use.

Finally, feel free to visit my Parents' Computer Companion Web page at `http://www.ccde.org/publications/pcc.html` or drop me an e-mail note at `jdb@loyola.edu` with any questions you may have. Please share with me any of your favorite computer activities or programs that you think others should know about. I'm always interested in assisting parents as they seek to harness the computer for their children's education.

Glossary
of Computing Terms

Adobe Acrobat—A popular software application used for transferring exact copies of documents.

ADSL—Asynchronous Digital Subscriber Line. A high-speed communications protocol that can be used for fast Internet connections.

AGP—Accelerated Graphics Port. A high-quality video interface, found in multimedia computers, that enables fast rendering of 3-D graphics.

AOL—America Online. The most popular Internet Service Provider.

authoring—Software programs used for the design and development of computer programs, Web pages, musical scores, and the like.

bounced mail—An e-mail message that is returned to the sender, usually due to an error in the destination address.

browser—An interface program that allows access to the World Wide Web. Microsoft Internet Explorer and Netscape Navigator are the most popular.

C++—A computer programming language.

cable modem—A high-speed modem that enables a computer to connect to the Internet through a cable television line.

CD-ROM—Compact Disc–Read Only Memory. A high-capacity optical storage medium.

chat room—A place to engage in text-based real-time online conversation. The Internet equivalent of a telephone party line or conference call.

CrossingGuard—An Internet filtering program sponsored by CrossWalk.

CrossWalk—A popular Christian portal found at `http://www.crosswalk.com`.

Cyber Patrol—Internet filtering software.

discovery—Software programs in which the student takes a journey of exploration.

domain name—The part of an Internet address (to the right of the @) used to identify an Internet-attached computer system. Examples include `aol.com`, `whitehouse.gov`, and `regent.edu`.

download—To electronically copy a file from a remote computer to a local one.

DSL—Digital Subscriber Line. A high-speed communications protocol that can be used for fast Internet connections.

DVD—Digital Video Disk or Digital Versatile Disk. A high-capacity optical storage medium that is more advanced than CD-ROMs. DVDs can hold music, movies, and computer data.

edutainment—Software programs that combine educational instruction and entertainment.

e-mail—Electronic mail.

hardware—A computer and its associated peripherals.

hard drive—A hardware component used to store computer software.

home page—A World Wide Web document containing text, graphics, sound, video, or hypertext links.

iMac—The latest Internet-ready line of Apple Macintosh computers.

Internet—An international computer network (actually, a network of networks) with over 60 million users.

Internet2—The second-generation Internet, currently under development, designed for much higher data transfer speeds than the current Internet.

Internet filtering software—Programs that restrict access to pornographic and other offensive online information.

IRC—Internet Relay Chat. A type of online chat room.

ISDN—Integrated Services Digital Network. A high-speed communications protocol that can be used for fast Internet connections.

ISP—Internet Service Provider. A company that provides connections to the Internet.

Javascript—A programming language used to enhance World Wide Web sites.

Juno—A free e-mail service.

KidDesk Internet Safe—A program used to child-proof a computer as well as block offensive Internet sites.

lapware—Software specifically written for infants.

listserv—An automated mailing list management program. Commonly used as a generic term for an electronic mailing list.

Mac—Nickname for an Apple Macintosh computer.

mailing list—A topical discussion held through e-mail.

MHz—Megahertz. A measurement of speed used with microprocessors.

microprocessor—A chip that serves as the brain of a computer.

Microsoft Internet Explorer—A graphical World Wide Web browser.

modem—A hardware peripheral that allows computers to communicate through a phone line.

multimedia—The computer use of sound, graphics, and video. A multimedia computer typically comes equipped with a sound card, CD-ROM drive, and speakers.

Netscape Navigator—A graphical World Wide Web browser.

newsgroup—A topical discussion group that functions like an electronic bulletin board.

online—A generic term used to describe the Internet and computer networks.

PC—Personal Computer. A term typically used to refer to IBM-compatible systems.

PCI—Peripheral Component Interconnect. A high-speed interconnection system found within newer computers to improve performance.

PDF—Portable Document Format. The document formatting standard used by the Adobe Acrobat software product.

Pentium—The brand name given to the current series of Intel microprocessors. The Pentium series includes the Pentium, Pentium II, and Pentium III chips.

plug-in—A small piece of software that is downloaded and coupled with your Web browser to support additional features such as streaming audio.

PnP—Plug and Play. A type of peripheral support designed for automatic configuration of new hardware thus eliminating cumbersome installation procedures.

portal—A site designed as an all-inclusive gateway to the Web. Portals typically are designed around a particular theme and often offer e-mail, chat and discussion areas, and links to help find information online. Yahoo and CrossWalk are examples of popular portals.

processor—A chip that serves as the brain of a computer. Also called a microprocessor.

RAM—Random Access Memory. The area where a computer stores data during processing.

Rated-G—An Internet Service Provider that filters and prevents access to offensive Web sites.

RealPlayer—A program that supports streaming audio and video.

reference—Software equivalents of dictionaries, encyclopedias, and other information repositories.

search engine—A program that allows you to search the World Wide Web by keyword.

shareware—Fully functional software freely available for download that can be evaluated first and purchased later.

software—The programs that run on a computer.

sound card—A hardware peripheral that enables a computer to produce high-quality sound.

streaming audio/video—A form of online audio and video broadcasting.

SurfWatch—Internet filtering software.

tutorial—Software specifically designed to take the place of an instructor and teach a particular topic.

URL—Uniform Resource Locator. The unique address given to each page on the World Wide Web.

USENET—A series of topical discussion groups found on the Internet. Groups are arranged in a hierarchical fashion with dotted names such as `rec.music.christian`. Used interchangeably with the term newsgroups.

username—An individual's account name on a computer system.

Visual Basic—A computer programming language.

Webzine—An online magazine published on the Web.

Web browser—An interface program that allows access to the World Wide Web. Microsoft Internet Explorer and Netscape Navigator are the most popular.

World Wide Web—A graphical Internet service containing thousands of magazine-like pages of information including text, graphics, sound, and video.

WWW—World Wide Web.

Yahoo—A popular portal, located at `http://www.yahoo.com`, that contains a subject directory of Web sites.

Jason D. Baker is an educational consultant at Loyola College in Maryland. He holds an M.A. in education from George Washington University and is currently pursuing his Ph.D. in communication at Regent University. His particular areas of interest are computer mediated communication and distance education. Jason, his wife Julianne, and their two sons live in Baltimore.

You can contact Jason by e-mail at jdb@loyola.edu or on the Web (`http://www.ccde.org/publications/pcc.html`).